Azorean Cooking

From my family table to yours

maria lawton

introduction

The Azores has such a special and magical place in my heart. Off the coast of Lisbon, Portugal lays an archipelago of nine Islands called the Azores. Each island is rich with diverse cultures, cooking and customs. But this cookbook is all about one island only: the island of St. Michael (Sao Miguel), also known as the Green Island as well as the largest island. It is on this Island of Sao Miguel that my family has lived for several centuries.

I was born in Sao Miguel in the village of Rosario, Lagoa to a wonderful family that has always surrounded me with lots of laughter, love and joy. I know I am truly blessed to have such wonderful memories, especially of my parents and my grandparents. Most of those memories have us gathered around our dining room table enjoying the most amazing meals. They would always consist of great food (always made fresh), great conversations and laughter, and great debates, since we all love to prove to each other that we are right!

As I worked on this journey of putting together this cookbook, it really became all about recreating those wonderful memories of my life with my family. The idea of putting a cookbook together came to me after my mom passed away. My mother was an amazing cook; her heart and soul was in all her meals and it was her way of showing us how much she loved us. Unfortunately, she never had any of her recipes written down. She did everything by sight and smell. The other problem was that she would only allow one of my older sisters to be with her in the kitchen at a time because she needed a lot of room and we couldn't get in her way. Since I was the youngest, I never got to cook alongside her. When I got older I wouldn't dare try to make her dishes knowing that I would be critiqued. Since it could never taste like hers, I just gave up. As a result, I concentrated on Italian cooking instead. I grew to love the whole process of cooking: the planning, the shopping, the prepping, the cooking, and the serving. My greatest return is to see the enjoyment in everyone eating my dishes. It's a feeling I can't explain—it brings me so much joy.

Sadly, it all changed when we lost my mom. After she passed I longed for her homemade meals. I wanted to recreate some of those food memories not only for me but for my children and one day my grandchildren. So at first, my sisters shared some of the recipes they had from my mom. Adeline had some of the soups and roast dishes while Isabel had the stuffing, the baked beans and a few desserts. Then, after our dad passed and we were cleaning out our parents' home, I found some actual recipes she had written in a spiral notebook. Thank goodness for my Aunt Lilia, who translated the recipes from Portuguese to English for me in addition to sharing the recipes she also had. It meant so much to me, even though I was still missing some recipes that I loved and longed for.

It was at that moment I really began to want to cook Azorean. I started my journey to learn all I could and to recreate and share all of my food memories with my family and friends. I started to look everywhere for Azorean cookbooks. While I did find cookbooks on Portuguese cooking, mainland cooking uses different spices and techniques than island cooking. Azorean cooking is highly flavored in spices such as safflower, cinnamon, malagueta hot peppers, paprika and bay leaf; we have so many influences in our cooking from Europe, Africa, India and the Muslim world. When I discovered that each Island has their own take on each dish, too, my goal was to find dishes I had grown up with—and all roads lead me back to Sao Miguel.

With my husband's support, I went back to visit my family in Sao Miguel and learned how to cook all my childhood dishes with my Aunt Ines (my dad's baby sister) as well as several of my cousins, Laureana, Helena and Daniela. One of the most emotional experiences came from cooking with my Aunt Ines. While we were cooking, her kitchen began to smell just like it would have if my mom had been cooking. We talked about my parents and how when my mom married my father she was not a very good cook. My dad would ask his mother to teach my mom some dishes, so it was no wonder that everything would smell the same so many years later: Ines and my mother had the same teacher! The smells were so overwhelming that I began to cry. It was as if I was cooking with my mom for the first time. From that moment on I knew my mom and dad were with me, and through this sometimes very emotional journey they have remained with me. I know they would be proud of me.

Putting together this cookbook took me longer than I imagined. At times it became very overwhelming for me. I found myself reliving everything all over again, and I would mourn the loss of my parents and grandparents with every memory of a celebration that we shared together. My parents and grandparents always celebrated life and loved life to the fullest. Through this effort I realized just how much I am like them. I am proud of who and where I came from. I am proud to be Azorean.

Yes, I am blessed. I am blessed for my beautiful family and for all the wonderful memories. It's these special memories we all have that stay with us forever, and I am so happy that I can share mine with you.

Sincerely,

Maria Lawton

This cookbook is dedicated to my parents and grandparents, who have always surrounded me with love that will always be with me, with the faith that all things are possible, and the hope that what we do will be passed on and never forgotten.

**A special thanks goes to all of you who helped reach my goal.
It started with a thought and you all helped me make it come true.**

My husband Bob and my daughters Erica, Rebecca and Sarah, who never lost faith.

My sisters Isabel and Adeline, who kept encouraging me.

My Aunt Lilia, who has always been there for me and helped me with cooking and translating recipes.

My cousins Laureana, Helena, Daniella and Cristina for the timeless help in researching family recipes.

My Aunt Ines, who let me in her kitchen and taught me to cook family recipes.

To my many taste testers: Claudia, Cynthia, David, Michael, Elizabeth, Karen and Ann.

To Jeremy Palmer, owner of CHIC Hair & Makeup Salon, for styling
my hair for the cover and all my important events.

To Steve Nunes & Steve Henriques, owners of
Imagemakers Photographic Artists, for taking the cover photo.

To Peg McGetrick, who allowed me into her home and be photographed in her amazing kitchen.

To all my family and friends, from the bottom of my heart I thank you.

Third Edition, 2nd Printing

soup

breads

entrees

desserts

other favorites

Soups

bread soup with mint and poached eggs

Açorda Sopa de pão com hortelã e ovo escalfado

When we were growing up my mom served this soup if you were feeling under the weather or just wanted something very light and simple for lunch or dinner. My fondest memory of this soup is from when my grandmother Filomena made it. She would say that this dish would give her strength, and after living to the wonderful age of 94 years, I would not argue it.

This recipe came from my Aunt Ines, who taught me how to make it. She explained that Açorda can be made simply by seasoning water with the spices and herbs you desire, and bringing it to a boil. Poach some eggs and place day-old bread on top, cover the pot and leave to the side until you're ready to serve. I remember my grandmother would make her Açorda with onion, garlic and mint. If you remember a different variation, the steps to make are the same; just follow along and substitute with your favorite ingredients.

Ingredients:

1 onion, finely chopped
1 garlic clove, sliced thin
1 tablespoon of olive oil
2 potatoes, peeled and chopped into cubes or slices
Salt to taste
Eggs
2 sprigs of mint (mint is used to infuse broth with taste and aroma, not to be eaten)
2 tablespoons of butter
1 loaf of day old bread, sliced

Directions:

In a medium stockpot, add enough water to fill half way. Add the potatoes, onion, garlic, olive oil and salt and bring the water to a boil. Reduce to a simmer and continue until the potatoes are cooked. Once they are cooked, break the eggs into the soup (one for each person served.) Once the eggs are cooked, add the slices of bread on top. Add the sprigs of mint on top of the bread, and finally add the pats of butter. Remove the pot from heat and cover. Let it rest for 5-10 minutes covered.

To serve the soup, remove the mint and discard. Ladle soup into each bowl, including enough of the broth with the bread, potatoes and one egg.

watercress soup

Sopa de Agrião

I grew up eating a lot of watercress soup in addition to kale or turnip green soup. It's a very delicate plant that doesn't take much time to cook. I remember my dad would plant several rows of watercress every spring. We would enjoy it fresh all summer long and my mom would freeze the rest for the winter. It's definitely a comfort food for me and one that I hope you will enjoy as well.

Ingredients:

10 cups of chicken broth
8 large potatoes, chopped
1 small onion, finely chopped
3-4 cloves of garlic
2 bunches of watercress, washed and picked off at the stem
Salt and pepper to taste
½ stick of butter
¾ cup of milk
*Lemon juice or olive oil to taste

Directions:

Using a large stockpot, add the chicken broth, potatoes, onion and garlic. Bring to a boil, then lower to a medium heat and cook until potatoes are soft and break easily with a fork. Remove the potatoes along with the garlic and place them in a separate large bowl Add the butter, milk, salt, pepper and mash together. Add the mashed potatoes back into the pot with the chicken broth and mix together. Let it simmer on low heat for a few minutes then add the watercress and cook for 10 minutes.

**You can also add pasta to the broth when you remove the potatoes, such as macaroni, and let it cook before adding the mashed potatoes back into the broth. You can also season each plate with fresh squeezed lemon juice or a drizzle of olive oil before serving.*

turnip greens soup

Sopa de Nabos

Growing up I thought that everyone had a garden. It was unthinkable not to have homegrown watercress, kale and turnip greens available for some of our everyday dishes. My father would make sure that every patch of dirt had some vegetable growing. So much was grown that we always had enough to freeze and use throughout our winters. It was very common for me to be asked to go in the garden and pick something for my mom's cooking. One of the soups she would often make used turnip greens since it was one of my dad's favorites. He loved it with fresh corn bread slathered in butter.

A couple of variations that my mom would do every once in a while would be to purée the potatoes in the soup as well as substitute butter for the olive oil. Also, for the pasta you can use what you have handy. Usually my dad would ask for macaroni shaped pasta instead of the stars.

Ingredients:
6 cups of water
1 large onion, finely chopped
2 garlic cloves, minced
3 medium potatoes, chopped in small pieces
½ cup of star-shaped pasta (or other small shape)
1 bunch of turnip greens, washed and chopped into small pieces
3 tablespoons of olive oil
Salt to taste

Directions:
In a medium stockpot add water, onion, garlic, olive oil and salt and bring to a boil. Add the potatoes, pasta and the turnip greens. Cover and cook until the pasta is cooked and the potatoes and greens are tender.

kale soup

Sopa de Couve

This kale soup recipe is the version I have made since I got married. I've always used my mom's recipe, since my new husband adored my mom's cooking and especially her soups. The thing with this soup is that there can be so many variations. Some kale soups might include variations such as beans, carrots, pasta and split peas that others don't include. The addition of these ingredients doesn't make the recipe right or wrong; it all comes down to how you prefer it or sometimes what you have available in your pantry. All I know is that I enjoy a nice bowl of it every once in a while and when I make it, it's this recipe I follow.

Ingredients:

1 fresh bunch of kale, washed, stems removed and rough cut
1 15.5 oz. can of red kidney beans, rinsed
1 large onion, finely chopped
2 carrots, chopped in bite size pieces
1 lb. of chouriço cut in half-inch rounds
8 cups of homemade chicken stock
4-5 potatoes, chopped in bite size pieces
Salt and pepper to taste
Olive oil

Directions:

Using a large stockpot over medium heat, add enough oil to cover the bottom of the pot. Add the onions and carrots and sauté until onions are translucent. Add the chouriço and cook for about 5 minutes. Add the chicken stock and the remaining ingredients and bring to a boil. Continue to cook on a low boil for 45 minutes to 1 hour. Add more broth, if needed. Just make sure if you do add more broth to season with more salt and pepper to taste. It's as easy as that…now time to enjoy it.

**Sometimes I don't want to have whole beans in my soup, so instead I cook the beans in a separate saucepan with some chicken stock and a little olive oil. Once the beans are cooked, I purée them and add it to the soup at the very end. I also do this sometimes with the potatoes as well. I love how just by doing this, the broth thickens a little and almost becomes creamy. It's delicious!!*

chicken and rice soup

Canja

My mom would serve Canja on special holidays and some Sunday dinners. She also made it when we were sick and needed something to give us strength, or at least that was the promise made for us to eat it. I know you must be thinking, "it's only chicken soup," but it's much more than that. Canja has a delicious creamy, lemony broth that will make you wonder why you've never had chicken soup like this before.

Ingredients:

1 organic 2-lb. chicken or 2 chicken breasts w/ bone
1 onion, whole and peeled
1 large garlic clove, left whole
1 cup of rice, rinsed
½ lemon, juiced
2 egg yolks
Salt to taste

Directions

Using a large stockpot over medium-high heat, place chicken in the pot and pour enough water in to fully cover the chicken. Add the whole onion and the whole clove of garlic. Cook for about 40 minutes, making sure to keep an eye on the water level and add more if needed. Once the chicken is cooked, remove the chicken, onion and garlic. Add the rice into the broth and stir.

While the rice is cooking, discard the onion and garlic and chop or shred the cooked chicken into small pieces. Place chicken back into the pot and stir well. Continue to stir until the rice is cooked.

Just as the rice is cooked, in a separate bowl beat together the two egg yolks with the lemon juice. Ladle a small amount of the broth into the bowl and mix together. This will temper the egg. Pour the bowl of tempered eggs into the soup and stir, allowing the broth to become a little thicker. Stir for a few minutes, then salt to taste.

To serve, just ladle soup into big bowls. If you're like my family, you will want to have a lemon nearby to squeeze some more fresh juice on top.

simple bean soup

Sopa simples de Feijão

This is a very simple bean lover's soup that my mom would make. She would always try to use dried beans instead of canned beans when making her soups. She felt the consistency of the canned beans was on the mushy side. In a pinch, though, she would always have canned beans ready for use in her pantry. The key to using dried beans is the soaking. It doesn't matter which bean you would like to use, the process is the same.

Measure out the amount of beans you would like to use and place them in a large enough bowl to be able to cover them with cold water and let them soak overnight. The next day, rinse the water out and make sure to remove anything that does not look like a bean. I'm saying this, because on a few occasions I've removed a very small stone! So, be careful and rinse thoroughly.

Ingredients:

3 cups of dried red or white kidney beans; be sure to soak them overnight
½ cup of olive oil
½ cup of chopped parsley
1 large clove of garlic, minced
2 cups of water, or more depending how thick or thin you like your soup broth
1 small sweet onion, cut in half
Salt and pepper to taste
1 tablespoon of the hot chopped peppers (optional)

Directions:

In a large stockpot add the olive oil, beans, onion, garlic, water and salt and pepper. Bring everything to a boil and then lower the heat and cook for 50-60 minutes. Keep an eye on the water and adjust as needed, until the beans are cooked.

Once the beans are cooked, remove about 1 cup of the beans along with the some of the broth and the onion. Using a food mill or blender, purée the mixture. Then add the mixture back into the stockpot, stir in the chopped parsley and the chopped red peppers and mix well. Simmer for another 10 minutes and taste the broth, seasoning with more salt if needed.

Serve over slices of Portuguese bread and a drizzle of olive oil on top.

carrot soup

Sopa de Cenoura

The first night when I returned to Sao Miguel, my cousin Laureana had made this soup for me. It was light and delicious and the perfect beginning of many more wonderful meals to come.

Ingredients:
8 cups of chicken broth or water
1 small head of cauliflower
6 carrots
4 medium potatoes
2 medium onions
Salt
Olive oil

Directions:
Chop all of the listed vegetables and place into a medium sized stockpot. Add the chicken broth and season with salt to your taste. Bring to a boil then reduce to a low simmer. Cover pot and cook until all the vegetables are cooked.

Once all of the vegetables are cooked you will need to purée them. You can do it two different ways: the old fashioned way is to remove all of the vegetables from the broth and have them go through a hand-cranked food mill. The second method uses a handheld food processor, stuck right in the pot. Whichever way you choose, the vegetables will be incorporated with broth to form a wonderful smooth texture.

When you serve this, the last thing you want to add is a drizzle of olive oil on top of each bowl of soup.

**A variation of this soup with more texture adds some chopped green beans or watercress after you have puréed the vegetables. Return to slow simmer until beans or watercress is cooked. Watercress takes hardly any time to cook and is my first choice to add when making this soup.*

pumpkin soup

Sopa de Abobora

Ingredients:

2 19-oz. cans of beans (I used red kidney beans) rinsed well or 1 cup of dried beans (if using dried beans, soak them in water overnight)
1 large sweet onion
3 large cloves of garlic
4 cups of water
2 tablespoons of tomato paste or 3 large tomatoes with skin and seeds removed
2 carrots, chopped
1 large white potato, chopped
2 large sweet potatoes, chopped
1 small pumpkin chopped and de-seeded (can substitute with butternut squash if pumpkins are not available, and be sure to save the pumpkin seeds so that you can roast them for a special crunchy treat)
Salt and pepper to taste
2 tablespoons of cinnamon
1 bunch of parsley, finely chopped
1 cup of pasta (optional)
Day-old bread, sliced (optional)
Olive oil (optional)

Directions:

Cook the beans, onion, garlic and water together in a large pot until onion is cooked (about 10 minutes) or until spoon can cut through the onion. Add the tomato paste or tomatoes and purée all the above using a handheld immersion blender. (My mom would use a hand-cranked food mill when making this soup; she liked the consistency of a thicker purée than you will get with a blender.)

Add all of the listed chopped vegetables into the purée and add enough water to cover everything. Season with salt and pepper to taste, then add the cinnamon. Stir it all together and simmer until pasta and potatoes are cooked. Be sure to keep an eye on the water level. If the potatoes are taking a while to cook and the soup is losing water, you can add hot water to restore the water level. Continue to simmer.

Once it's cooked you can serve. I usually like to serve my soup over a slice of day-old bread. The bread just soaks up all of the liquid and then I drizzle olive oil over it and enjoy every minute of the hearty soup. But there are no rules to follow…you can still serve over bread, or just use pasta and no bread. It's really up to you and what you're in the mood for.

roasted butternut squash soup

Sopa de Abobora Assada

This is a fall favorite in my home. When I was growing up my mom would always have some type of pumpkin, squash or sweet potato in our soups or with roasts as a side dish; fall would not be same without it. I am very lucky to have a brother-in-law that has a huge vegetable garden. Ernest always has an abundance of sweet potatoes and squash and I end up getting special deliveries at my back door. It's always a wonderful surprise and something I look forward to every September when I start making this soup. It's a creamy soup with chunks of roasted squash and a hint of cinnamon. Serve with crusty bread and a glass of red wine... perfect for a crisp fall evening.

Ingredients:

2 whole butternut squashes, split and de-seeded
2 19-oz. cans of beans (I used red kidney beans), rinsed well or 1 cup of dried beans (if using dried beans let them soak in water overnight)
5 carrots, roughly chopped
6 large sweet potatoes, roughly chopped
5 garlic cloves
1 large sweet onion, roughly chopped
3 tablespoons of cinnamon
Salt and pepper to taste
1 bunch of parsley, chopped very fine
Olive oil

Directions:

Preheat oven to 350° F.

Place the split and de-seeded squash face up on a roasting pan or baking sheet. Drizzle olive oil, salt and cinnamon over the squash and roast in the oven for about 1 hour or until tender. Once it's done, take it out of the oven to let it cool while preparing the rest of the soup. Once it's cooled enough to touch, peel the skin off and cut into bite-size cubes; set aside.

In a large stockpot add the beans, onion, garlic, carrots and sweet potatoes. Add enough water to cover all of the vegetables. Season with salt, pepper and cinnamon and bring the water to a boil. Then lower the temperature and cook until all the vegetables are cooked. Purée all of the vegetables in pot using a handheld immersion blender. You can also purée in batches by using a regular blender and or a food mill.

Once the soup is puréed, taste to see if it needs more salt, pepper and cinnamon. This soup has a tendency to be on the sweeter side, so you need to keep checking to adjust to your taste. Then finally add in the chopped parsley and the roasted squash into the pot and mix everything together.

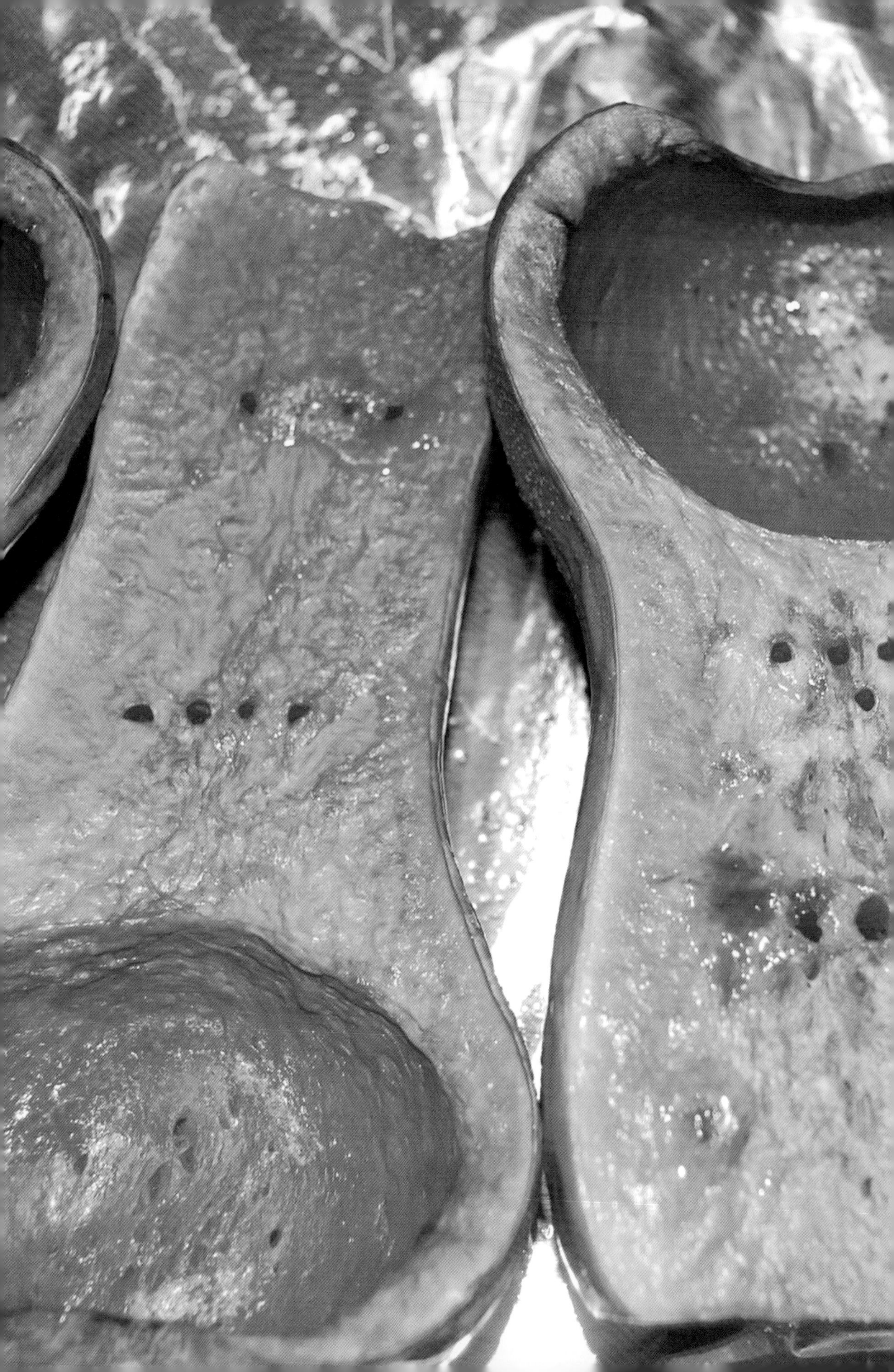

azorean

Breads

sweet bread

Massa Sovada

My Mom's Recipe

This recipe is what really started me thinking about collecting and putting my childhood recipes together. Before my mom became ill I asked her for her massa recipe. She gave me a list of ingredients with no step-by-step instructions and sent me on my merry way. She would always say it was a lot of work and that her daughters had no time for it; she was right at the time. Why would we attempt to make something that she made so well? She would make it for special holidays and events, and during the rest of the year we all patiently waited. But we knew as soon as she did make it we would all be around her like little children waiting for it to come out of that oven. Then some of us could not wait until it cooled down as she suggested and we'd just cut into it and enjoy each bite. The house would be so nice and warm and the sweet smell filled the air...it was heaven!

It took me several years after she passed before I even attempted to make her massa. It also took several more years of failed attempts until my sister Adeline remembered that when my nephew David was twelve years old he had helped my mother make her massa, something she never let her daughters do. Better yet, he even wrote down the steps that she herself never wrote down. He had forgotten all about it until that conversation with my sister. For that I am forever thankful to David!

This recipe makes 5 to 6, 9 inch round loaves.

Yeast:
3 ¼-oz packets of active dry yeast (I use Fleischmann's Rapid Rise)
4 tablespoons of flour
1 cup of warm water

Dough:
5 lbs of all-purpose flour
¾ tablespoon of salt
4 sticks (1 lb) of butter at room temperature
4 cups of whole milk
12 large eggs at room temperature
5 heaping cups of sugar

Egg wash:
1 egg

Directions:

The first step is to proof the yeast. In a small bowl dissolve the 3 packets of yeast and the 4 tablespoons of flour with a cup of lukewarm water. Mix together and set aside until the liquid becomes foamy and begins to rise. It usually takes about 10 minutes.

**If this does not happen after a good 20 minutes, your yeast might not be active and you will have to start again with new yeast.*

Next, heat the milk and butter in a large saucepan over medium to low heat. Stir frequently until the butter has completely melted. Let mixture get very hot, but not at boiling point. Set aside.

Then, in a large bowl, use a hand mixer to beat together the eggs and sugar. Start at low speed, then once it's incorporated raise the speed to high so that you can whip the mixture until it becomes light and fluffy and air bubbles start to form. The mixture resembles a light batter and when left standing for a minute, foam should form at the top. Set aside.

Pour the 5 lbs of flour into a very large bowl, then sprinkle the salt over it. Form a well with the flour by pushing the flour to the sides of the bowl. Add the egg and sugar mixture into the well and with a wooden spoon start mixing it all together. Then very slowly add the milk and butter mixture. Continue to mix and once all of the milk and butter has been added, the dough might be getting harder to mix with the spoon. If that happens at any point you'll need to start kneading with your hands. Once everything has been mixed or kneaded well, lastly you'll add in the yeast to the dough.

Knead the dough really well, using a slight slapping and hitting motion. Check at all times for lumps, since lumps are not wanted. Once well-kneaded, cover the dough in the bowl and let it rest for a half hour.

After the half hour has passed, knead the dough again, bringing the sides of the dough up to the middle and punching it down again. Continue that for several times before sprinkling the top of the dough and sides of bowl with flour. Cover the bowl of dough with towels and sometimes blankets to keep warm and away from drafts. Let the dough rise until it doubles in size. This can take awhile, sometimes up to 4 hours.

Grease the baking pans (9 inches in diameter, 3 inches high) well with butter and set aside. Once the dough has doubled in size, flour your hands first then punch down the dough, kneading it several times. Constantly flour your hands lightly before you grab the dough and rip off appropriate sized pieces. Knead in hands into a ball-like shape and place in baking pan. A large baking pan can take up to 3 balls of dough. After placing all of the dough in each greased pan, let it rise while covered again in a warm, draft-free spot until doubled in size, about 2-4 hours.

Preheat oven at 325° F. Position the rack in the middle of the oven and make sure to remove any extra racks.

Once the dough has doubled, use a pair of sharp scissors or a knife to make a shallow slash across the top of the dough in a cross design. Then create an egg wash by beating one egg and brushing it generously over the top of each loaf. Bake for 45 to 60 minutes or until golden brown. Test with a toothpick; it should come out clean when it's done but make sure to watch it closely and don't over bake the sweet bread or else it will become too dry. Transfer to a rack to cool for 20 minutes then remove the sweetbread from the pans and let cool completely. You can wrap each well in plastic and it will last for 2-3 days.

Note: The only time when these steps change is during Easter. When sweet bread is baked during Easter season, raw eggs in their shell are placed in the dough just before baking. This is meant to be a symbol for life and rebirth. We call the Easter Sweet Bread with eggs a "folar". The difference in making would be to set aside a large grapefruit-size piece of dough after the first rising period to create strips. Then later, instead of slashing a cross design, you would insert the raw egg or eggs on top of the dough, pressing them in, and with the extra dough place 2 small strips over the egg forming a cross design. Then you would brush the egg wash over the top of the loaf before placing in the oven.

sweet bread

Massa Sovada

My Tia Lilia's Recipe

Here's a sweet bread recipe that my Aunt Lilia gave and taught me. One of the reasons I love this recipe is that I can make a small batch of 2-3 loaves instead of the usual 6 loaves. Also, because it's a smaller batch I can use my KitchenAid stand mixer to do a lot of the mixing before it needs to be kneaded by hand. She also taught me that if I decide I want to make sweet bread on a cold day, to make sure that the kitchen is nice and warm. She kept saying, "You don't want the bread to catch a cold or else it will take all day for it to rise!" So, I make sure to turn the oven on first thing in the morning to help give the room extra heat and that seems to do the trick. Also, the night before you're making the sweet bread, be sure to remove the eggs and butter from the refrigerator and have them sit out to warm up to room temperature.

This recipe makes 2 to 3, 9 inch round loaves.

Dough:
2 ½ lbs of all-purpose flour
3 cups of sugar
8 large eggs
3 sticks (3/4 lb) of butter
2 cups of milk
1 lemon zest

Yeast:
3 ¼-oz packets of active dry yeast (I use Fleischmann's Rapid Rise)
4 tablespoons of flour
1 cup of warm water

Egg wash:
1 egg

Directions:
Proof the yeast by dissolving the 3 packets of yeast and the 4 tablespoons of flour with a cup of warm water. Mix together and set aside until the liquid gets all foamy and it begins to rise, about 10 minutes.

Heat the milk and butter in a saucepan over low heat. Stir frequently until the butter has completely melted. Then set aside to cool until it is lukewarm.

Then, in a large bowl, beat the eggs, sugar and lemon zest until it's creamy and light.

Using a stand mixer fitted with a dough hook and on speed #2, add into the bowl in this order: yeast, milk and butter mixture, egg and sugar mixture and then slowly add the flour about ½ cup at a time until everything is mixed together well, about 10-15 minutes.

**If you do not have a stand mixer, use a large bowl with a wooden spoon and follow the same directions as above. When it gets to hard to mix with a spoon, use your hands and continue to mix then knead the dough. If dough is still a little wet, you can add a little more flour.*

Place the dough in a larger lightly buttered bowl, cover well with tea towel and let rise in a warm, draft-free spot until it doubles in size, about 2-3 hours.

Grease the baking pans (9 inches in diameter, 3 inches high) and set aside. Once the dough has doubled in size, punch down the dough, knead it several times and form it into 2 or 3 balls. Place each ball into their greased pan and let rise covered with a tea towel, in a warm, draft-free spot until doubled in size again, about 2-3 hours.

Preheat oven at 325° F. Position the rack in middle of the oven and make sure to remove any extra racks.

Once the dough has doubled, use a pair of sharp scissors or a knife to make a shallow slash across the top of the dough in a cross design. Then create an egg wash by beating one egg and brushing it generously over the top of each loaf. Bake for 45 to 60 minutes. Test with a toothpick; it should come out clean when it's done but make sure to watch it closely and don't over bake the sweet bread or else it will become too dry. Transfer to a rack to cool for 20 minutes, then remove the sweet bread from the pans and then let cool completely. You can wrap each well in plastic and it will last for 2-3 days.

Note: Another method my aunt taught me to proof the yeast uses a boiled sweet potato. After it's been boiled, peel the skin and remove all veins. Mash it and let it cool completely. Add 3 packets of rapid rise yeast, 1 tablespoon of flour and enough warm milk to form a batter. Then leave aside and let rise for about 10 minutes. By using this method it gives the sweet bread a distinctive color, almost a light orange. The sweet potato does not alter the taste at all.

portuguese pancakes/ yeast cakes

Bolos Lêvedos

Make no mistake about it: these are not your typical pancakes. They are closer to what I call the Azorean version of the English muffin. So whether you call it muffins or pancakes, you can't go wrong. I remember when I was young having these delicious treats made by Rosalina Pimentel, a very sweet and beautiful woman who was the mother of my brothers-in-law Ernest and Denis. Who knew after all these years I would find her recipe tucked away in a spiral binder with a note from my mom saying that these were her favorite?

They are a very special treat to make because they are fairly time-consuming. I am very lucky that these pancakes can be easily found in my neighborhood supermarket, made and delivered by a local Portuguese bakery, because they really can take all day to make! But, of course, I had to try and make them myself. This recipe tastes delicious, and there is certainly a big difference in flavor compared to the store-bought version, making this a recipe worth trying for special occasions.

This recipe makes a lot of pancakes – approximately 2 dozen – and can be easily cut in half. The whole batch is too much for my husband and children to share, but the other taste testers in my family, including my sisters and nieces, were very happy to take some off my hands!

There is nothing better than warm Bolos Lêvedos with some hot tea or coffee. Then the following day, you can cut them in half and toast them. Serve them with butter and some jam, or with fresh cheese. I hope you try them and enjoy them as much as we did.

Ingredients:

3 ¼-oz packets of active dry yeast (I use Fleischmann's Rapid Rise)
1 cup lukewarm water
3 heaping cups plus 3 tablespoons sugar
5 lbs all-purpose flour
12 eggs
2 cups whole or 2% milk
2 sticks (1/2 lb.) butter
1 tablespoon salt, dissolved in 1 tablespoon of warm water
1 lemon rind, grated

Note: The butter and eggs should be at room temperature, so take them out of the fridge at least a few hours in advance.

Directions:

Dissolve the yeast packets in lukewarm water (not too warm or it will kill the yeast). Stir in 3 tablespoons of sugar. Mix well and leave aside, allowing time for the yeast to proof.
In your mixing bowl, add eggs and the 3 cups of sugar. Mix until the color is a light cream and the consistency is just as creamy. Set aside.

In a sauce pan over low heat, add milk and butter, stirring until butter is melted and milk is warmed. Set aside.

In a very large bowl, add flour and create a well in the center. Pour the melted butter and milk into the well and mix with the flour. Add lemon zest and salt, continuing to stir. Add the creamed eggs and sugar and continue to mix well. Don't be afraid to start using your hands if the mixture is too hard to use the mixing spoon. Then, add the yeast that has proofed. Mix together, and knead the dough for 15 minutes in the large bowl.

Then cover the bowl with a cloth and leave aside until the dough rises. (Hint: To help the dough rise faster, I usually turn on my oven to add a little more warmth to the kitchen, and then place the covered bowl on the counter next to the oven.) It usually takes 2 hours for the dough to rise.

After the dough rises, begin to take pieces of the dough out of the bowl and roll in your hands, forming balls the size of a medium orange. Make sure you dust your hands with flour as you do this since the dough is sticky.

Place the balls of dough on a floured cookie sheet and dust lightly with flour before covering with a cloth and allowing them to rise a second time, usually 4 hours.

After the dough rises, take each ball of dough and pat them down with flour-dusted hands to shape them to the desired size.

Dust a cast iron skillet with flour. (Resist the urge to use oil – I know it sounds funny, but trust me!) Set the stovetop temperature to low to medium heat. If it's any hotter, the flour (and muffins) will burn.

Place the flattened dough on the skillet one at a time and allow it to slowly cook, turning it occasionally to make sure it doesn't burn. Use a toothpick to test and see if it is cooked through.

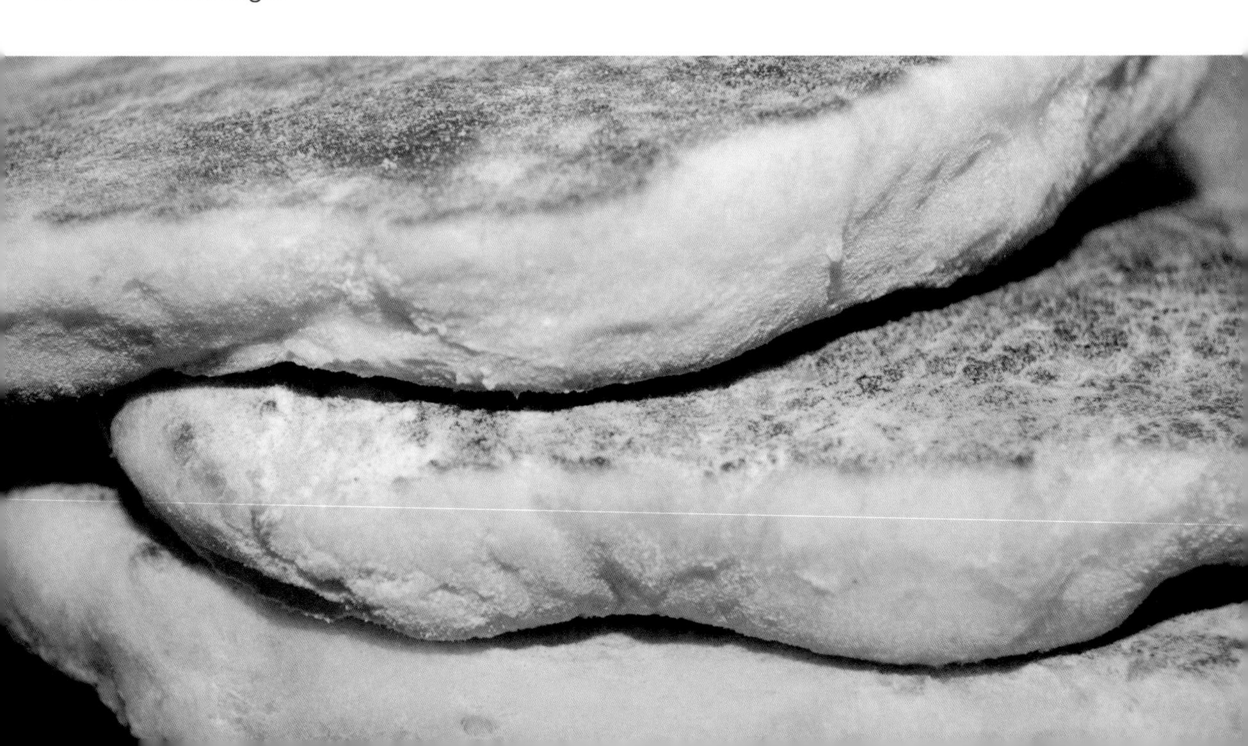

homemade bread

Pão Caseiro

Pão Caseiro means "bread made at home". They're usually large-sized, rustic round loaves with a crispy outside crust and a soft texture on the inside. Growing up in the U.S. my mom would bake bread only once in a blue moon. We were very lucky to live just a very short walking distance to a wonderful Portuguese bakery so almost every day we had fresh baked bread in our home. We would always have popo-secos (Portuguese pops) and Vienna bread during the week, but on the weekend the bakery would make corn bread and Pão Caseiro. My mom explained that to make a great tasting Pão Caseiro you really need to have a yeast sponge made and ready to start the bread. She said that when we lived in Sao Miguel she would bake bread everyday, so she would always have a yeast sponge ready in her kitchen cabinet. Of course when we would have these conversations, I had no idea what she was taking about and no recipes were ever exchanged. All I remember her saying was "it was lots of work".

Many years after my mom's passing I found myself sitting at my Aunt Ines' kitchen table in Sao Miguel and learning every step of baking Pão Caseiro from her; this is the same recipe my mom would have made. The key to the recipe was having yeast made a day ahead of time and saved until it was needed. Using this method gives the bread a better texture and flavor than your usual bread. The breads were also baked in fire-heated stone ovens but I don't have a bread oven in my kitchen. I have found that by using a large pizza/baking stone for the bread to bake on top of, the bread can have a crispier, outer crust.

This recipe makes one loaf, but it can be easily doubled.

Ingredients for the yeast sponge:
1 cup of lukewarm water
1 teaspoon of active dry yeast
2 cups of all-purpose flour

Directions for the yeast sponge: (To be made the night before baking your bread)

Using a large bowl, pour in the water and yeast and mix well. Then stir in the flour and make sure everything gets mixed well together. Cover the bowl with a couple of tea towels and keep in a draft-free area to let the yeast ferment overnight.

Ingredients for the dough:
1 cup of lukewarm water
1 teaspoon of active dry yeast
3 very full cups of all-purpose flour
3 teaspoons of salt
Pre-made yeast sponge

Directions for the dough:
In a large bowl, pour the water and active dry yeast and whisk well together. Add in the yeast sponge and stir together. Add in the flour a little at a time and stir together until it becomes too hard to handle and you must use your hands to mix. Remove the dough from the bowl on to a floured surface and use your hands to continue to knead the bread for at least 5 minutes or until the dough feels smooth and elastic to the touch. If the dough is too soft, add a little more flour; if it's too dry, add a little more lukewarm water.

Grease the large bowl with softened butter and add the dough back in. cover it with a couple of tea towels and let it rise in a draft-free place until the dough has doubled, usually about 1 to 2 hours.

After the dough has doubled in size, remove it from the bowl and place onto a floured surface. Start shaping the dough by punching it and deflating it. Keep kneading the dough and create a large circle out of it. Once it's at the shape you're happy with, place the dough on a floured surface, cover it, and let it rise again until it doubles in size. That takes about 1-2 hours.

About a half hour before the dough is ready, preheat the oven at 400° F. Move the rack to middle of the oven and remove any extra racks. If you're using a baking stone, place it in the oven now to allow it to become nice and hot. Then when the dough is ready, transfer the dough onto the center of the stone. If you are not using a baking stone, place the ready dough on a floured baking pan instead. Using a very sharp knife slash a cross on the top of the loaf and bake for 50-60 minutes.

You can test to see if bread is baked by removing the bread and tapping on the bottom; if it sounds hollow it's done. Transfer loaf onto rack and let it cool.

portuguese bread rolls

Papo Secos

This very easy recipe was given to me by my Aunt Lilia. She heard me complain about my other attempts at making bread and how long it took me. With promises that this recipe would be different, making just a small quantity of 10 pops, I gave it a try. I am so glad I did, because in just two and a half hours I had fresh rolls done and out of the oven. If you have never made bread before, you should start with this recipe.

Ingredients:
4 cups of all-purpose flour
2 teaspoons of salt
2 teaspoons of sugar
1 1/4 oz. envelope package of rapid rise yeast
2 cups of lukewarm water
1 egg white, beaten, or milk for brushing

Directions:
Using a large bowl mix together the flour, salt and sugar then leave aside.

In a separate large mixing bowl, add the two cups of lukewarm water and gently mix in the yeast using a whisk. Add the dry ingredients into the water a little at a time and keep mixing until it forms a soft ball of dough. At this time you will need to use your hands to mix in the remaining flour and combine together. Place the dough onto a floured surface and knead for a couple of minutes. Place the dough into a greased bowl and cover with a dish towel or blanket. Move the bowl to a warm place and let the dough rise for an hour.

Remove the dough and place onto a floured surface again. Punch the dough down and knead for about 10 minutes, until the dough feels smooth.

Separate the dough into ten equal balls. Shape them and place them on parchment paper-lined baking trays, and let them rise for 30 minutes. You can shape the rolls by making an indent in the middle with the side of your hand, or you can roll the dough into an oval shape and score with a knife across the top lengthwise before it goes in the oven. Whatever way you choose you really can't go wrong.

Preheat the oven at 375° F and brush the rolls with either egg white or milk. Bake for 30 minutes or until the rolls are slightly golden brown and sound hollow when tapped on the bottom.

You'll be very tempted to eat them hot out of the oven, but let them cool off for a few minutes before you do. Enjoy!!

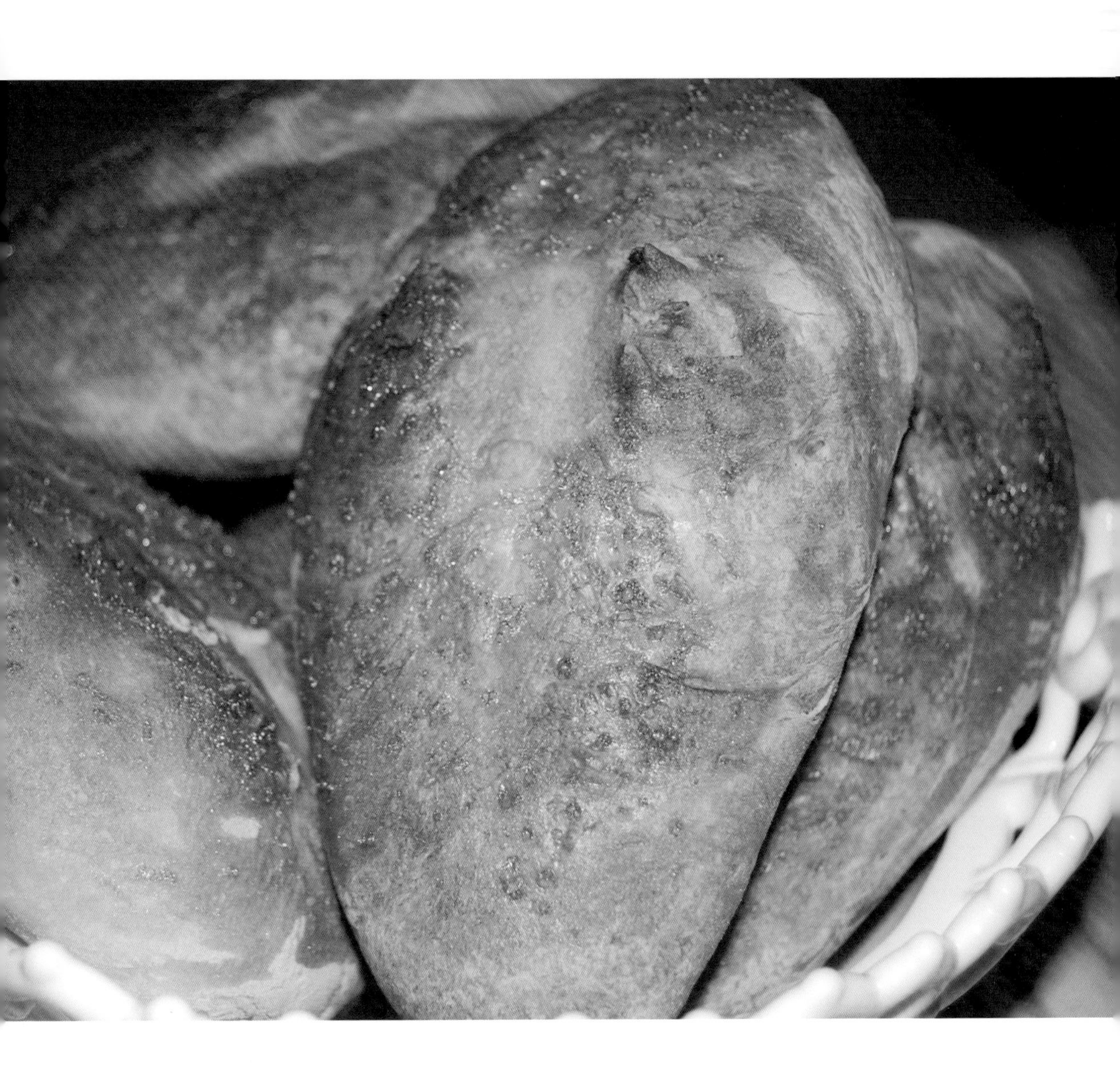

white bread

Pão de Farinha de Trigo

The idea of making bread kind of scared me; the thought of it seemed out of reach and I imagined it being so much harder then it really is. I am so happy that this was the recipe I started with; it really is so simple to make. The recipe makes 4 loaves, but can be easily halved. This recipe was given to me by my cousin Helena, and it's one that I have made quite often and can't imagine not making it!

Ingredients:

4 lbs of all-purpose flour
3 cups of lukewarm water
2 tablespoons of salt
4 tablespoons of sugar
2 1/4 oz. envelope packages of rapid rise yeast
4 tablespoons of softened butter
2 eggs, beaten
1 cup of canola oil

Directions:

In a large bowl, add the water, salt, sugar and yeast. Using a hand mixer mix everything well together. Then add the butter, oil and eggs and continue to mix until everything is well incorporated. Then add the flour a little at a time still using the hand mixer until it becomes too hard to handle. At that time you will have to mix and knead the dough by hand, adding a little water to the dough if it's too dry. If it becomes too hard to knead in the bowl, transfer the dough to a floured surface and continue to knead.

Once it's all mixed, put the dough back in the bowl and cover it with some tea towels and let it rise in a warm draft-free place till it doubles in size. It usually takes 1-2 hours.

Once the dough doubles in size, place the dough onto a floured surface and cut the dough into 4 equal sections. Knead each section and shape the dough into loaves. You can either bake the dough in greased bread loaf pans or freestyle onto a parchment-lined baking tray. Using a sharp knife cut a straight line on top of each loaf and let it rise again for 30-45 minutes.

Then place in preheated oven at 400° F and bake for 1 hour. The bread will become a deep golden brown color on top. A great way to also know if the bread is done is to take the bread and tap the bottom; if it sounds hollow, it's done!

**I sometimes take the bread out of the loaf pans 15 minutes before they're done and put them back in the oven to bake on a tray instead. That way all sides get a little golden color.*

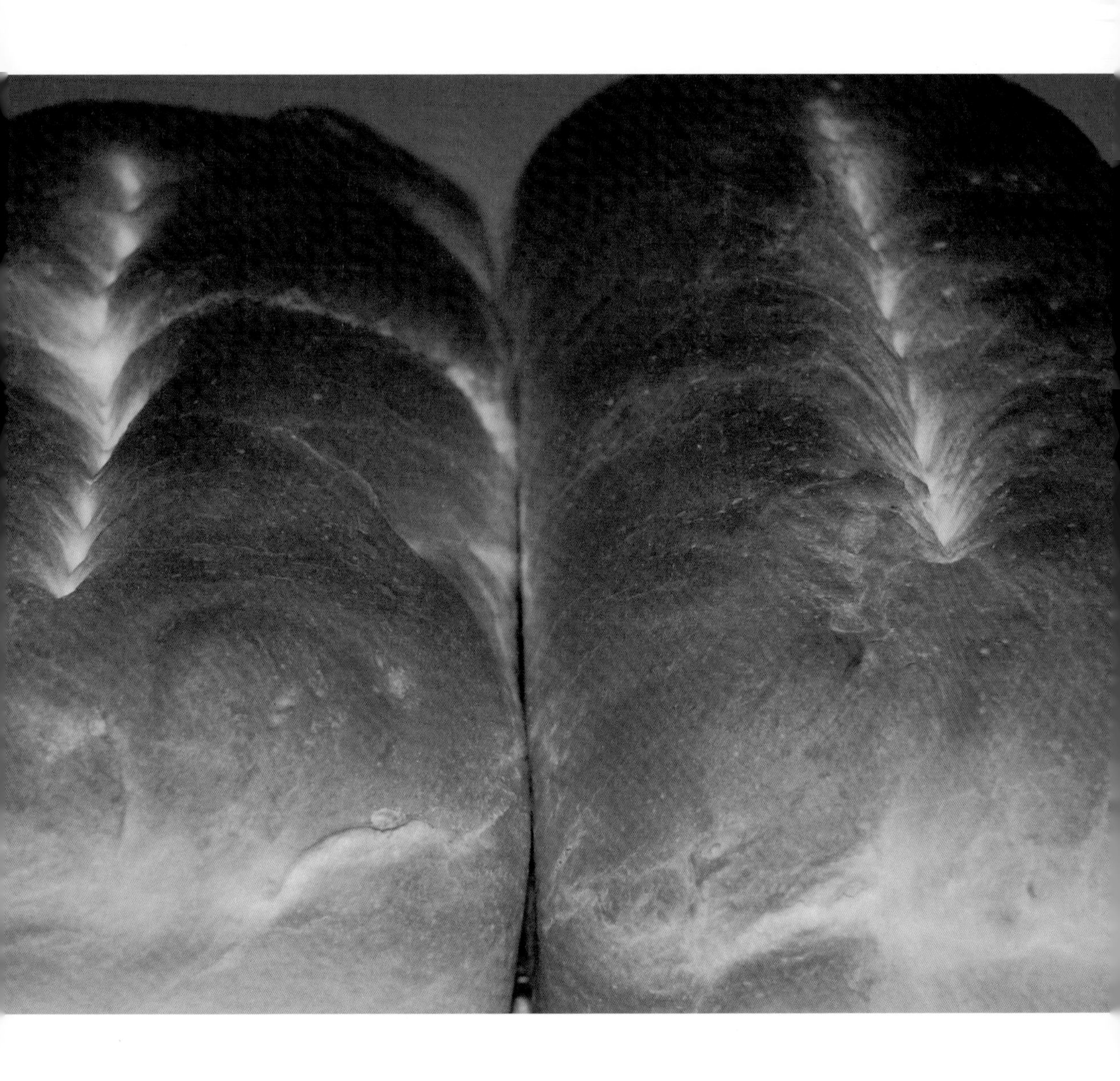

portuguese corn bread

Pão de Milho

This recipe was given to me by my Aunt Lilia. I experimented with several different recipes, but this one came out the best for my taste. It was crusty on the outside and soft on the inside. My whole family and I love to eat it fresh out of the oven with lots of butter slathered on it.

Recipe makes 1 loaf

Ingredients:
1 1/2 cups white corn flour
1 1/2 teaspoons salt
1 cup boiling water
1 1/4 oz. package active dry yeast
1 tablespoon of butter or oil
1 teaspoon white sugar
1/4 cup lukewarm water
2 cups all-purpose flour

Directions:
In a small bowl, sprinkle yeast and sugar over the lukewarm water. Let stand for 2 or 3 minutes, and then stir to dissolve. Set the bowl in a warm, draft-free place for 8 to 10 minutes, or until yeast doubles in volume.

In a large mixing bowl, combine 1 cup corn flour, salt, and boiling water. Stir vigorously until smooth. Cool mixture to lukewarm. Stir proofed yeast into the cornmeal mixture. Gradually add the remaining corn flour and all-purpose flour. Knead and gather the dough into a ball, and place it in a greased bowl. Cover, and set it aside in a warm place for about 30-45 minutes, or until doubled in size.

Grease the bottom and sides of a 9-inch baking pie pan with 1 tablespoon olive oil or butter. Turn the dough out into pie pan, and cover. Let it rise in a warm place for another 30 minutes, or until it doubles in size again.

Bake bread in the middle of a preheated 350° F oven for 40 minutes, or until top is golden. Transfer to a rack to cool.

flat skillet cornmeal bread

Bolo da Sertã

This bread was made by my mom almost every week. It is great alongside kale soup, a boiled dinner, or grilled fish. The great thing about this type of bread is that there is no yeast in it so it can be made very quickly. The other great thing is that it's all cooked in a cast iron skillet.

This recipe will make 3 skillet breads.

Ingredients:

2 cups of white corn flour
1 cup of all-purpose flour
3 tablespoons of sugar
1 tablespoon of salt
1 tablespoon of baking powder
2 cups of boiling water

Directions:

In a large mixing bowl add the corn flour, salt and sugar. Add the boiling water very slowly, stirring until it's well mixed. Then mix in the all-purpose flour and baking powder. Adjust the dough by adding more water or flour depending on the dough feeling too dry or too wet. Separate into 3 equal parts and pat down each one to size. Leave to side to rest.

Using a large cast iron skillet, make sure not to grease or oil the pan; instead, you will dust the skillet with flour. Place the bread into the hot skillet then lower the heat and make sure to keep turning the bread over often not to burn, until it is cooked.

You can test if it's done by inserting toothpick in the center; it should come out dry.

Entrees

hake stew

Abrótea Guisada

This dish has a very special place in my heart. My mom and dad both loved this and it was one I took for granted when I was growing up. After they both passed, it was one of those dishes I craved but after trying to recreate it and failing every time I really thought I would never have it again. Then on my trip to Sao Miguel I mentioned this dish to my Aunt Ines and she informed me that her mom, my grandmother, was the one who taught my mom the recipe. It was one that my aunt still made and was ready to teach me. You cannot believe how happy I was to hear this, and could hardly wait for the cooking lesson. What happened during and after the lesson was very moving to me. I was so happy to finally taste and smell a dish I thought was lost that all I could do was cry. Yes, I cried while cooking it and I cried while eating it. It's hard to explain, but I felt like I was with my parents at that table, enjoying each bite.

Recipe serves 6

Ingredients:

3 lbs of fresh Hake, scaled, gutted and cut into 2 inch potions
**Hake is in the cod family, but if you can't find it you can substitute with red snapper*
2 large onions, sliced
4 scallions, chopped
1 tablespoon of crushed red hot pepper sauce
2 tablespoons of tomato paste
¼ teaspoon of pure safflower (Assafroa)
**can be picked up in international cooking aisle or Portuguese markets*
1 small bunch of parsley, chopped
1 lemon
4 tablespoons of olive oil
Salt to taste

Directions:

In a dutch oven, add the onions and scallions and add 2 cups of water; bring to a boil for a few minutes. Strain out the water completely from the pan, leaving the onions and scallions.

Add the olive oil to the pan and sauté the onions. Add the red hot pepper sauce and the tomato paste. Then add water and the fish, making sure the water covers the fish. Add the safflower, and salt to taste. Bring the water to a boil and continue until the fish is cooked. When the fish is cooked, add the chopped parsley and squeeze the lemon juice over the top.

To serve, place a serving of fish with the broth over a slice of day-old bread. The bread will soak up lots of the broth, so make sure to add extra broth to each dish.

salted cod

Bacalhau Salgado

Because our islands are surrounded by the Atlantic Ocean, fish has always been in abundance and a big part of our diet.

Bacalhau is a salt-preserved codfish. Salted cod is mostly sold as cod fillets that have been heavily salted to draw out the moisture to preserve it and then air-dried. I'm not going to go into the history of it or give you directions on how to salt and hang them on the clothesline, but I do remember seeing that in some yards when I was very young as well as in the fish markets around the corner from my home. I would see my parents picking out these large fillets for our Friday night dinners. Sometimes my mom would make codfish with rice but more often she would make a salted cod dish consisting of boiled cod and potatoes with a parsley sauce over it. It was a staple in my home, but when I married and tried making the same dish I was very intimidated for quite a few years by the whole process of cooking with it. I thought I could substitute it with fresh cod and no one would know better; boy, was I wrong! The flavors cannot be compared; salted cod has a slightly salty, more intense flavor than fresh cod. Once I got past my fears I realized it was a very simple process. So if you haven't cooked with salted cod, here are my helpful hints on preparing it and getting ready for a wonderful dish.

When purchasing salted cod make sure to pick out a piece that has a thick center. Avoid the fillets that contain more tail than anything else as that part is so flat and has very little meat. Also, check to see if the cod has bones or not. I prefer the boneless and skinless portions, but note that it usually costs more for that convenience. Some people will disagree and say that salted cod with bone has even more intense flavor. I personally don't notice a difference in flavor, but you can experiment and decide for yourself.

Once you have the dry salted cod at home, you need to have the cod soaked in water overnight or to a full twenty-four hours, depending on the thickness of the fish as well as your preference of a salty flavor. Since I like it fairly salty, I usually do the overnight routine. I rinse the salt off it first, then I place the salted cod in a bowl large enough to hold the cod well. Then I pour cold water to cover the cod completely. Soak the cod for 12 or more hours, depending upon its thickness (refrigerate it in hot weather), changing the water 2-3 times daily. On the last soak before cooking, you can substitute milk for water. This last step is important: both my mom and my aunt would say that using milk for the last soaking will make the cod more moist. And I agree. When I have done it by just soaking it in water the cod is not as moist or as flaky.

I hope this helps you and now you're ready to cook some delicious salted cod dishes.

SEM
Espinha
799:L
Bacalhau
Noruega
$7.99Lb

cod fish à gomes sá

Bacalhau à Gomes de Sá

This codfish recipe is the most traditional dish. As far as I can remember, my mom would make this dish for us. Plus, this is the first dish I attempted to make when I was learning to cook with salted cod. If you have never cooked with salted cod, I recommend starting with this recipe. I've been told that since there are more than 1,000 recipes for cooking cod this one particular recipe has several variations. When I visited my family my cousin Joao Manuel's wife Anna Paula made me Bacalhau à Gomes Sá, Sao Miguel Style. This method added layers of green and red peppers as well as white wine in the layers. So if you're feeling adventurous go right ahead and try different layers. But first we are starting with the basics.

Ingredients:

1-2 lbs dried salted cod, soaked overnight and rinsed several times (I prefer skinless and boneless cod)
6 medium potatoes, peeled and kept whole
2 large onion, sliced thin
3 cloves of garlic, sliced
6 tablespoons olive oil
3 eggs, boiled
Black olives
I small bunch of parsley, chopped
Salt and pepper to taste

Directions:

Prepare the cod the day before by using the soaking method described on page 38.

In a large pot, boil the cod then remove it. If you didn't buy it skinless and boneless you can now remove the bones and skin and splinter it crudely and leave to the side.

Add the potatoes to the boiled water and parboil them. You don't want to overcook the potatoes or else you'll have a hard time cutting them in slices after. Once the potatoes are parboiled and sliced, and leave them aside.

In a separate saucepan hard-boil the eggs, peel them and cut them into slices and leave aside.

In a frying pan, sauté the onions in olive oil until they are a golden color. Add the garlic and cook together for a few minutes.

Preheat the oven at 350° F. In a baking or casserole dish, alternate layers of potato slices, cod and onions until you use it all up. Make sure to drizzle a little olive oil on every layer. Place in the oven and bake until golden on top.

Finally, garnish with olives, sliced eggs and chopped parsley.

salted cod with a white sauce casserole

Bacalhau salgado com um Ensopado de Molho Branco

Ingredients:
1 lb of dry salted cod
4 medium carrots
8 large potatoes
2 onions
3 cloves of garlic
1 chouriço sausage
3 hard-boiled eggs
1/2 cup of olive oil
1/2 cup of chopped parsley

White sauce:
4 cups of milk
2 tablespoons butter
2 tablespoons all-purpose flour
Salt and black pepper to taste

Add the butter to melt, add the flour and stir. Mix in the milk gradually and whisk together. Bring to a boil, and let boil for about 5 minutes. Season with salt and pepper and cover the cod.

Preparation:
Prepare the cod the day before by using the soaking method described on page 38.

In a large pot, boil together the soaked cod, carrots and potatoes. Once cooked, skin and pick out the bones of the cod, and shred it into medium pieces. Cut the potatoes and carrots into slices and leave everything aside until you're ready to use. In the meantime, using a smaller pot, boil the eggs and the sausage together. Once cooked, remove and peel eggshells, and after they've cooled off, slice the eggs. Do the same for the chouriço sausage, removing the casing and slicing it into small rounds before leaving aside.

In a large frying pan, sauté the onions with garlic in the olive oil until onions are a golden color, then leave aside.

Grease a baking dish that is at least 3 inches in depth, then start to assemble the layers: first the onions, then the potatoes and carrots, then the shredded cod. Repeat the layering until you use up all of the ingredients. On the final top layer place the slices of eggs and chouriço. Then, cover with white sauce and place in a 350° F oven and bake until sauce starts browning. Add a top layer of chopped parsley for decoration and color before serving.

cod fish croquettes

Pastéis de Bacalhau

This recipe came from my Aunt Lilia. Every first Sunday after Christmas, my aunt and uncle John have an open house at their home that lasts from noon until the last person leaves. They have been doing this for as long as I can remember and it's wonderful to see extended family as well as friends who you haven't seen all year. This event takes a lot of planning and a lot of cooking. Every room has a purpose...the dining room has all the desserts, the TV room has all the snacks, and the kitchen has the rest. I know that I look forward to this event every year for many reasons; family, laughter and great food are the top three! There are a few dishes that my aunt makes that I know will be there and I always know it will be delicious. This is one of them...

Ingredients (makes approximately 50 croquettes):
6 large regular white potatoes
2 lbs of salted boneless codfish
3 large eggs, separated
Salt and pepper to taste
1 bunch of parsley finely chopped
1 large sweet onion finely chopped
4 garlic cloves, minced
1 heaping tablespoon of all purpose flour
½ gallon of milk for soaking cod
4 tablespoons olive oil
Light olive oil, for frying

Preparation:

Prepare the cod the day before by using the soaking method described on page 38.

Peel and cut the potatoes into large cubes and place them in a large pot filled with water. Cook the potatoes until they are parboiled, then add the cod fish to the same pot and cook together with the potatoes until the cod fish is cooked. This should take about 15 to 20 minutes, depending on the thickness of the cod. Once cooked, the cod will flake easily when poked with a fork. After it's cooked drain into a colander and let cool. Place the potatoes into a large bowl, and mash the potatoes really well. Set aside. In a separate bowl shred the cod fish by hand into very small pieces. Set aside.

In a small skillet, heat olive oil over medium heat and sauté the onions until they are a golden color, then add the minced garlic and cook for a minute more. Add this mixture into the bowl of mashed potatoes, then add the shredded cod to this bowl, mix well and taste. It's really important to taste at this stage to see if the cod is still salty enough for you. It all depends on your taste whether you season the mixture with more salt or not. Then, stir in the 3 egg yolks and the heaping tablespoon of flour and mix well.

In a medium bowl, whip the egg whites to soft peaks and fold into the cod mixture.

Heat oil in deep frying pan or a quart pan and make sure to fill the pan halfway with light olive oil. Make sure not to overheat the oil or the croquettes will burn very quickly.

Use 2 large tablespoons or serving spoons depending on the size croquette you want to have. Use one spoon to scoop the cod mixture and one to make the shape. You can also use an ice cream scoop if you want them in a ball shape, but the small football shape is what I have always been accustomed to. Add the croquettes into the oil and fry until golden brown, about 2 minutes. Fish out the croquettes with a slotted spoon and place them on a paper-toweled plate. You can at this point, sprinkle some salt over them while they're still very hot.

You can serve them hot, warm or at room temperature on a platter and decorate with a sprig of parsley on top and lemon wedges on the side. Everyone will love them.

**If you like them spicier you can add 1 tablespoon of chopped red hot pepper sauce to the mixture before frying.*

oven roasted sea bass

Pargo Assado no Forno

I was served this wonderful dish when I visited my family in Sao Miguel. It makes a great entrance and display on the table, which makes sense since they also call this fish the "emperor of all fish". My cousins told me that cod will always be king, but this fish is quickly becoming everyone's favorite. This recipe comes from my cousin Laureana's husband Fernando.

I am very lucky to live close to one of the largest fishing communities in the United States. When I purchase fish I buy from a local fish market that owns its own fishing boats. The fish is extremely fresh, plus they will scale and gut the fish for me. I recommend you get to know the fishmonger in your community; it makes buying fish so much easier.

Ingredients:

4 lb sea bass, whole (cleaned and gutted)
2 onions, chopped
3 garlic cloves, sliced
3 tomatoes, sliced
1 small bunch of parsley, chopped
Salt to taste
Olive oil
Crushed red hot peppers, to taste
White wine
2 bay leaves
1 lemon, juiced

Directions:

Preheat oven to 400° F.

In a large roasting pan, line the bottom of the pan with 1 chopped onion. Arrange the whole sea bass on top of the onions and pour enough wine to cover a few inches up the sides of the roasting pan. Pour enough olive oil to cover the fish and have the seasoning adhere to it. Add the remaining ingredients surrounding the fish as well as stuffing the fish.

Place into oven uncovered, and cook for 20-30 minutes. Making sure to baste the fish with the liquid in the pan every 10 minutes or so.

Once it's cooked, a great way to serve this dish is with a side of boiled potatoes and a green salad. Make sure you place the fish on a large tray and spoon some of the pan liquids along with the cooked ingredients on top of the fish, and decorate it with some sliced lemons and some sprigs of parsley. Your guests will be very impressed.

fresh cod poached in onion, garlic tomato sauce

Bacalhau Fresco Escalfado com Molho de Tomate, Cebola e Alho

This recipe is a very simple and quick fish dish that can be made with any type of white fish. I prefer using fresh cod or hake and I always buy half a pound of fish per person, because I like to serve ample portions to my guests.

Recipe serves 4

Ingredients:
2 lbs of fresh cod fish, cut into portions
2 lbs of ripe tomatoes, peeled, seeded and chopped
2 large sweet onions, sliced and cut in half
4 cloves of garlic, thinly sliced
6 tablespoons of olive oil, or enough to cover the bottom of the pan
1-2 tablespoons of the chopped hot pepper sauce
2 cups of white wine
Salt and pepper to taste
1 tablespoon of paprika
1 small bunch of parsley, chopped

Directions:
Heat the oil in a large, deep skillet over medium heat. Add the onions and cook until they turn a nice golden color, about 15 minuntes. Next, add the garlic and mix well with the onions. Then add the chopped tomatoes with their juices, wine, salt and pepper and the hot chopped pepper sauce. Stir everything together thoroughly, then lower the heat and simmer everything together for about 30 min. You'll notice that the tomatoes will break down and the sauce will begin to thicken.

At this point you can start to add the portions of fish and lay them on top of the tomato sauce. Season the fish with salt, pepper and paprika, and sprinkle the parsley on top. Use the lid to cover the pan for about 5-10 minutes or until the fish is cooked to your liking. The steam will poach the fish faster than you think, especially if the fish is a thinner fillet, so keep a good eye on it.

I love to serve this dish with a nice green salad, some fresh bread and a great glass of wine. Enjoy.

fried horse mackerel with villain sauce

Chicharros Fritos com Molho Vilão

Looking back, I always remember my dad being the one who was at the grill frying up the fish. My parents would pick up the Chicharros at the fish market and then clean, scale and gut these little fish while always leaving on the head and tail. Then they would dredge them in corn flour and fry them until they were nice and crispy. After grilling they were so crispy that we would eat the whole fish in just a few bites.

When I visited my cousin Laureana her husband Fernando made this recipe for me. He wanted to bring me back to those wonderful memories of eating outside in the summer under the grape arbor. Those days were long ago, but eating this dish always brings me back. I like to serve the mackerel with boiled potatoes covered in the sauce along with stewed fresh fava beans.

This recipe serves 4

Ingredients:
2 lbs of clean, gutted and scaled Horse Mackerel
Corn flour for dredging
Oil for frying
½ cup of table wine
½ cup wine vinegar
1 cup of olive oil
1 onion, chopped fine into thin slices
2 cloves garlic, crushed and finely chopped
1 hot red pepper cut into thin strips*
*can substitute with 1 tablespoon of chopped red hot pepper sauce
1 bunch of parsley, chopped
Salt and pepper to taste
1 teaspoon of safflower or paprika

Directions:
Season the mackerel with a little salt and then dredge them in the corn flour, making sure to shake off the excess flour. Place them into a hot frying pan, and fry them until crispy and a golden brown color. Note: my family always fries these outside on the grill because they have a really strong odor.

Meanwhile, prepare the sauce to either pour over your fish or serve on the side.

In a bowl add the chopped onion, garlic, pepper and salt. Add wine, vinegar and olive oil. Mix everything together and let it all rest a bit before adding parsley and safflower.

Taste and adjust the seasoning as needed. You may want to add more olive oil or vinegar along with some salt and pepper.

shrimp mozambique

Camarão Moçambique

This recipe was originally given to me by my sister Adeline. Since then it has become a staple dish in my home. I love to serve it as an appetizer as well as the main dish. When serving as the main dish I serve the shrimp over a bed of butter rice or a slice of day-old homemade bread. The bread soaks up the wonderful sauce and it's sheer heaven to eat.

Ingredients:

4 tablespoons butter
2 tablespoons of olive oil
2 sweet onions, chopped
1 cup water
8 garlic cloves, chopped
4 tablespoons chopped flat leaf parsley
2 envelope packets of Goya saffron seasoning "Sazon Goya con Azafran"
1 ½ cup white wine or more, depending on how much sauce you would like
Juice of 1 lemon
Salt and white pepper to your taste
2 teaspoons hot crushed red peppers (or generous pinch of the dried crushed red pepper)
2 lbs of shrimp, peeled and de-veined (26-30 count)

Directions:

Using a 3-quart pot or large, deep skillet, melt the butter over medium-low heat, add olive oil and sauté the onions until they turn a little golden in color.

In a separate bowl, dissolve the saffron packets with a cup of water. Pour the water into the skillet followed by garlic, crushed red pepper, parsley, salt and pepper. Cover and simmer for 3 to 4 minutes, allowing the spices and herbs to mingle well together.

Pour in the white wine and squeeze in the fresh lemon juice. Stir. Cover and raise heat to medium-high and bring the sauce to boil for a few minutes. Then reduce the heat to medium-low.

Toss in the shrimp and cook for three minutes over medium-low or until the shrimp turn pink in color.

Spoon the shrimp into bowls and serve with plenty of crusty bread to dip in the delicious sauce.

periwinkles cooked in a wine sauce

Caramujos Cozidos em Molho de Vinho

The first memories I have of eating periwinkles are from when I was young and my family would spend our summer Sundays at the beach. It was a whole day event, and it included my grandparents, my aunts, uncles, and several cousins, and that doesn't include my own family. My grandfather would organize all the children to find periwinkles and fill up a pail. As soon as our pails were full we had to bring them to the camp fire where all the women were preparing a great meal. Then, after more playing on the beach, we were all called back to eat. That's when I would see my grandfather in all his glory. He really enjoyed eating the periwinkles. He would use a toothpick or a pin to pick them out of their shell, and then he would dunk some bread into the sauce and wash it all down with a nice glass of red wine. Those were wonderful times with my family that I will never forget, and for that reason I wanted to share this recipe in honor of my avô and padrinho. This recipe came from Aunt Lilia, who was one of the many women who prepared this dish for him.

Ingredients:

3 lbs of periwinkles or snails
2 quarts of water
2 cups of white wine
Olive oil
1 medium onion, chopped
3 cloves of garlic, chopped
Small bunch of parsley, chopped fine
2-3 tablespoons of crushed hot red pepper sauce; depending on how spicy you like it
1 teaspoon of paprika
Salt and pepper to taste

Directions:

As soon as you get the periwinkles home, make sure to wash them in a colander under cold running water. Peek at the opening of each to make sure that the covering is securely shut. (It's a sign that they are still alive.) Smell the ones that might look like they are missing that covering, which might mean that they are dead. If you detect an odor other than salt water, discard those pieces.
After washing them well, leave to the side.

In a large sautéing pan over medium heat, add enough olive oil to sauté the onions until they are translucent. Add crushed hot pepper sauce, paprika, garlic and salt and pepper to taste. Stir all together and add the water and wine, then bring to a boil. Once the broth is at a boil add the chopped parsley, and finally add the periwinkles. Stir everything together and cook for 3-4 minutes. They cook very fast, so keep a close eye and don't overcook them.

Ladle them out into a big bowl and enjoy it with some crusty bread and great wine!

baby clams in a wine, onion and garlic broth

Amêijoas Num Molho de Vinho, Cebola e Alho

Ingredients:
4 lbs of baby clams or littleneck clams
1 bunch of scallions, chopped
1 bunch of parsley, chopped
1 small onion, chopped
2 tablespoons of hot chopped pepper sauce (or more depending on how spicy you like it)
4 cloves of garlic, chopped
2 tablespoons of paprika
Salt and pepper to taste
Olive oil
White wine
Water

Directions:
Soak clams overnight in water with salt and corn flour. This process will remove the sand from inside the clams. The clam will actually spit out the sand.

Heat the oil in a deep-sided sautéing pan and sauté the scallions and onions until onions are translucent. Then add the garlic, parsley, hot pepper sauce and paprika and stir until well combined.

Add 3 cups of water and about 2-3 cups of white wine and bring to a boil. Taste the broth and add salt and pepper to your taste. At this time add the rinsed baby clams to the pan, making sure that there is enough liquid to cover the clams. If needed add more wine. Lower the heat and cover the pan for about 15 minutes. Uncover the pan and the clam shells should all be opened.

Discard any clams that didn't open; now you're ready to serve them.

Make sure you have lots of bread for dunking in the broth... It's simply delicious!

boiled dinner

Cozido

My mom served a boiled dinner for our Sunday lunch at least once a month when I was growing up. She knew it was one of my dad's favorite meals, and it also leaves plenty of leftovers for the week. We knew she would turn the stock into a soup. Then, after a few days, whatever was still left would get mixed with eggs and turned in to several tortas. We would stuff these into fresh pops to have amazing sandwiches. After my mom passed it was my two older sisters, Isabel and Adeline, who knew how to make my mom's boiled dinner. They had helped her in the kitchen and each remembered different steps. So it was wonderful to have them teach me.

Ingredients:

3 lbs of beef shanks with meat
2 lbs of pork shanks with meat
1 lb of pork ribs cut in half
½ lb of fresh bacon back, in one piece
1 lb of chouriço
1 lb of blood sausage (morcela), wrapped and tied in cheese cloth
1 bunch of fresh kale, clean and stems cut
1 small cabbage, cut into wedges
6 potatoes, peeled and cut in half
1 large onion, whole
2 sweet potatoes, peeled and quartered
4 carrots, peeled and cut in half
2 bay leafs
¾ cups of rice, rinsed and placed in rice ball
**My mom would cook rice in the boiled dinner by using a rice ball. The broth cooks the rice and makes the rice take on all the flavors of the dinner, and the mint brings it to another level of taste.*
2 springs of mint, placed in rice ball

Direction:

The night before, you will need to salt the bacon back, pork shanks and ribs and leave them covered in the refrigerator. Season the beef shanks separately with salt, pepper and a little cinnamon and also refrigerate overnight.

The following morning, fill a large stock pot halfway with water and add all of the meat. Over medium heat bring to a boil and cook until all the excess fat raises to the top of the pan. Then remove all meat out of pan and discard the water.

Clean the pan and refill halfway with water again, and add the meat, chouriço, bacon back, bay leaves, and onion, and cook until meat is tender and you can stick a fork right through it, about 1-2 hours. Since the morcela doesn't take that long to cook, wait to add it until about a half hour before the meats are cooked. (The reason it's cooked in the cheese cloth is that the casing on it is very thin and sometimes burst while cooking.)

Once all of the meats are cooked, remove from pan and set aside. Add the carrots, potatoes and the rice ball and bring the broth back to a boil, then reduce to a simmer and cook for 20 minutes. Add the cabbage, cut side down, and the kale last and continue to cook for 30 minutes. If you run out of room in the pot, have a separate pot and fill with broth from the larger pot and cook some of the vegetables separately.

The boiled dinner is served on several trays: one for the meats, one for the vegetables, and one for the rice.

boiled dinner in furnas

Cozido das Furnas

One of the many places everyone needs to see when visiting Sao Miguel is the village called Furnas. Besides being able to take a warm mineral bath and visit the beautiful Botanical Garden you must have the cozido. This "boiled dinner" is placed underground in a natural steam pit and your dinner will be cooked by volcanic vapor. It's a sight and taste you'll never forget. Simply amazing!!

roast beef

Carne Assada

When I was growing up my mom would make a roast beef dinner occasionally for one of our Sunday dinners, especially in the colder months. She would marinate the beef the day before, and then on the next day it would go into the oven and the whole house would fill up with this wonderful aroma. We felt it took forever to roast, even though it actually was only a few hours, but the wait was always worth it; the meat was so tender and flavorful. To this day, I also make this dish for my family and I hear them say the same words I used to say: "Is it almost done? It smells so good, Mom!" I love seeing that the tradition continues.

Ingredients:

5 lbs of 7 bone chuck roast or bottom round
1 lb of chouriço, chopped in quarters
2 onions, sliced
6 carrots, peeled and chopped in half
6 potatoes, peeled and chopped in quarters
2 tablespoons of crushed red hot pepper sauce
1 tablespoon of cinnamon
1 tablespoon of paprika
3 garlic cloves, sliced
2 cups of red wine or burgundy
Olive oil
¼ cup butter (half of a stick)
Salt and pepper to taste

Directions:

Make sure to marinate the beef the night before. Place the beef in a large container and cover with wine, garlic, onions, cinnamon, red hot pepper sauce, salt and pepper. Make sure the meat is well covered with marinade, then cover the container and store in refrigerator overnight.

The next morning preheat the oven at 350° F. In a large bowl add the carrots and potatoes, then drizzle with olive oil and season with salt, pepper and paprika. Mix the vegetables to make sure they get coated with all the seasoning. Leave to the side.

In a large roasting pan add the marinade, place the beef in the center and surround it with the seasoned potatoes and carrots, making sure to pour the remaining seasoned oil over everything. Add the chouriço in between the vegetables and the beef, then cut up the half stick of butter and scatter the pats of butter over the beef. Cover the pan and cook for 2 hours. Uncover and continue to cook for another 30 minutes.

skewered meat

Carne de Espeto

This recipe comes from my sister Adelina. For many years she worked at a restaurant in New Bedford called The Portuguese Shanty. The restaurant was owned by two sets of her in-laws, the Pimentels and the Pontes. The cook was Joe Ponte and this dish was one of his signature dishes. For many years, especially at family cookouts and to everyone's delight, Joe would always bring this Carne de Espeto dish. For all those years we would try to get him to share with us his secret ingredients until finally one day he shared it with my sister Adelina. It seems so simple, but the secret ingredient is the Burgundy wine. Trust me, you have not had skewered meat as tasty and tender as this. Thanks Joe for sharing this wonderful dish!

Ingredients:
5 lbs of top sirloin tips
4-6 tablespoons of garlic powder
4-6 tablespoons of onion powder
3 garlic cloves, sliced
2 onions, roughly chopped
Burgundy wine (enough to cover the meat)
Kosher sea salt and black pepper to taste

Directions:
Mix all ingredients in a large container, cover and marinate overnight in the refrigerator.

When you're ready to cook, thread the chunks of meat onto skewers and cook to desired doneness on the grill.

You can serve the meat on a bed of rice or you can also serve it my favorite way, stuffed in a Portuguese roll.

marinated pork butt

Caçoila

This very easy recipe for cacoila came from my Aunt Lilia. The funny thing about cacoila is that it's a staple in so many of our homes but most of us buy it already made from our local Portuguese meat markets or bakeries. Some are seasoned a little differently, but in the end what we have is sheer goodness. It's almost considered our fast food, always there for a quick lunch or dinner. My family's favorite way to eat it is by having the cacoila shredded and stuffed in a fresh baked pop (Portuguese roll).

Serves 4

Ingredients:
3 pounds of pork butt, cubed (for less fat, can substitute with pork loin)
1 onion, chopped
2 tablespoons of crushed red hot peppers (can substitute with red pepper flakes)
1 cup of white wine
2 tablespoons of paprika
1 teaspoon of kosher sea salt
1 tablespoon of wine vinegar
2 bay leaves
4 garlic cloves, chopped
1 tablespoon of cinnamon
½ cup of olive oil, for sautéing

Directions:
Make sure to marinade the pork at least one day before cooking. In a large container, add the cubed pork and mix in the red hot peppers, wine, paprika, salt, garlic, cinnamon, wine vinegar and bay leaves. Mix everything together, making sure the pork is covered well in the marinade. If needed you can add a little more wine. Cover the container and leave in the refrigerator until the next day.

The following day, remove the pork from the marinade, making sure to save the marinade to the side. Using a dutch oven, heat the olive oil over medium-high heat and sauté the chopped onion until it turns opaque or translucent. Add the pork and brown the meat. Once the meat is browned, add the reserved marinade and cook at a simmer for about 1 ½ hours or until the meat is tender.

To serve you can have the cacoila with a side of buttered rice and some vegetables, or you can shred the pork and serve as sandwiches. Either way your family will be happy.

fried pork belly

Torresmos Brancos

My mom would fry up some pork belly called Torresmos brancos for my dad and then fry up some blood sausage called Morcela and serve it with fresh corn bread. Being very young I didn't appreciate it as much as I do now. Now I love nothing better than all of the above served with fried eggs for a hearty breakfast. My family also loves the Torresmos; I mean, who wouldn't love fried crisp pork belly (aka fresh bacon)! That said I still can't get them to even try the blood sausage; it could be we need to change the name for starters. I debated whether to include this recipe in the book because it's just so simple. But for most of us we still buy them at the Portuguese meat market in their pre-cooked section because we don't have the time and need the convenience. But for those of you who want to attempt making it here it is. A warning to those who do make it: it's very addictive! There I said it, now I don't feel so bad about sharing.

Ingredients:

2 lbs of uncured fresh pork belly from a butcher shop. Have the butcher make sure he gives you a piece that also contains a certain amount of meat in it too. Have him slice in strips for you as well. This will make it easier for you to cut in pieces after.

Directions:

Cut the pieces of pork belly into one inch pieces.

In a large deep skillet over medium heat add all the pieces in a single layer and season with salt and pepper to taste. As the pork belly begins to fry in its own fat, make sure to continually stir the pieces so that each side is crispy. If you have a splatter screen, now would be the time to use it as it does tend make a mess. You can also lower the heat to lessen the splatter as well. Once it's to your desired crispiness, use a slotted spoon and place the fried pork belly on top of a paper toweled covered tray.

Once they are done, what you have is crispy goodness of fried pork belly to be enjoyed by all!!

tomato sauce with onions and eggs

Ovos Com Molho de Tomate e Cebola

This recipe was one of my favorites especially during the summertime when we would have an abundance of tomatoes in our garden. My mom would always make this for our lunch and we all looked forward to it. It was always served with crusty bread or grilled corn bread. Sometimes she would add more onions than tomatoes and called it a cebolada and it would accompany a meat or a fish dish. Either way it was always amazing. I find myself making it for my lunch as well as my dinner. Even during the off season of garden tomatoes I know I can substitute with canned or boxed tomatoes, but you cannot beat the flavor of the fresh summer tomato.

Ingredients:

4 lbs of ripe tomatoes, peeled, seeded and chopped
5 large sweet onions, sliced and cut in half
4 cloves of garlic, thinly sliced
6 tablespoons of olive oil, or enough to cover the bottom of the pan
1-2 tablespoons of the chopped hot pepper sauce
Salt and pepper to taste
4-6 eggs

Directions:

Heat the oil in a large dutch oven pan over medium heat. Add the onions and cook until they turn a nice golden color, about 20 minutes. Add the garlic and mix well with the onions. Then add the chopped tomatoes with their juices, salt and pepper and the hot chopped pepper sauce. Lower the heat and simmer everything together for about 30 minutes. You'll notice that the tomatoes will break down and the sauce will begin to thicken. At this point you can start to crack your eggs on top of the sauce. You can base how many eggs to break by the number of people you're serving. I personally like 2 eggs just for me, so I make sure I know who wants what before I start cracking them open. Use the lid to cover the pan for about 5 minutes or until the egg is cooked to your liking. I like my eggs over medium so 5 minutes works well for me but if others like it a little runny, less time is needed.

To serve, I spoon out the sauce into a bowl and place the eggs on top. Alongside it I have some crusty fresh bread or grilled corn bread. My favorite is to scoop up the tomato and onion with the bread with a little egg on top… I can't explain it, but it is so delicious and simple.

stewed green beans with chouriço and poached eggs

Feijão Verde Guisado Com Chouriço e Ovos Escalfados

This dish was a summer staple in my home when the garden was filled with lots of green beans. Sometimes my mom would also make it using fresh peas and fresh fava beans. I love it no matter which fresh vegetable is in season. It's a very simple dish to make, and one you'll have as a standby when you need to serve those quick meals.

Ingredients:

2 lbs of fresh green beans, cleaned and cut
1 medium onion, finely chopped
1 lb of chouriço or linguiça
1 tablespoon of crushed red hot pepper sauce
Salt and pepper to taste
4 tablespoons of olive oil
Eggs

Directions:

Using a dutch oven pan, add enough olive oil to cover the pan; over medium heat sauté onion. Once the onions have become translucent add your sausage (chouriço or linguiça) cut up into rounds and sauté them for 5 minutes; add salt and pepper to taste (as well as a spoonful of hot red crushed pepper if you like it hot!). Now add the fresh green beans and stir together. Next, add enough water to cover the beans and bring to a boil, then lower and simmer until the green beans are cooked to your liking and the water has evaporated.

The final step is to crack one egg per person over the top of the stewed green beans. Cover the pan and remove it from the flame to let the eggs cook in the steam (you're poaching the egg). Let it poach to your liking: some people like their eggs a little runny, so it's up to you for how long to keep the eggs covered and poaching.

I enjoy this dish with some fresh crusty bread and a nice glass of wine.

roasted chicken

Frango Assado

This recipe came from my mom who showed me how to make it soon after I got married. I wanted to impress my new husband with a roasted chicken dinner, and my mom came to my rescue. That was one of the great things about living on the second floor of a triple-decker, with my mom and dad on the first floor and my sister Isabel and her family on the third: I knew if I needed any help someone would be there. To this day, it's a go-to, easy recipe for the weekend. Even my oldest daughter when she comes to visit will ask me days in advance to make it for her when she arrives. It's one of our favorite comfort foods in our home.

Ingredients:

6-8 lbs roasting chicken, cleaned and rinsed
1 lb of chouriço or linguica cut in quarters
4-5 potatoes, peeled and cut into quarters
4-5 carrots, peeled and cut in half
6 cloves of garlic, chopped
1-2 tablespoons of the chopped red hot peppers **adjust to taste on how spicy you like it.*
2 onions, chopped in quarters
2 tablespoons of paprika
1 lemon
Olive oil
Salt and pepper to taste

Directions:

Preheat oven at 350° F.

In a large roasting pan, add chopped onions to line the bottom of the pan. Place the chicken on top of the onions and stuff some of the onions into the cavity of the chicken. Cut the lemon in half and squeeze the lemon juice over the chicken, then add the lemon halves into the chicken cavity as well.

In a separate bowl add the potatoes and carrots and add olive oil and some salt, pepper and paprika. Toss everything together, making sure that the vegetables get well coated. Place the potatoes and carrots around the chicken and make sure to add all the seasoned oil over the vegetables. Next, pour some more olive oil over the chicken, add the hot red peppers and some paprika and rub all these seasonings around the chicken, making sure not to miss a spot. Add the garlic and the chouriço or linguiça in between the chicken and the potatoes and cover the roasting pan and roast for 2-2 ½ hours. In the last 15 minutes, uncover the chicken and cook to give the chicken a nice golden color.

corn bread stuffing

Recheio

This recipe came from my Aunt Ines. This is the same recipe my mom would make to go with stuffed mackerel or to accompany a roasted chicken or turkey dinner. The only difference when making the poultry recipe was the addition of chicken or turkey liver and giblets to the ingredients.

It really is very versatile and can accompany any meat dish. It has a good kick with the chouriço and hot red pepper sauce and you can adjust it to your taste. Also, make sure that you're using bread that is at least 1 to 2 days old, truly the older the bread the better. You can also substitute with any bread, so if you don't like cornbread, just double up with the white or bread of your choice.

Ingredients:
1 Portuguese corn bread
1 loaf of white bread **I prefer Vienna Bread*
3 eggs
2 cups of milk or chicken broth
1 pound of chouriço cooked and shredded
1-2 tablespoons of hot red pepper sauce, more or less to your taste
½ teaspoon of paprika
1 bunch of parsley, finely chopped
1 medium onion, finely chopped
2 garlic cloves, chopped
Salt and pepper to taste
Olive oil

Directions:
Cut both breads in to pieces and remove the crust if it's too hard. Place the pieces of bread in a large bowl and leave aside.

In a small saucepan, place the chouriço and enough water to cover, bring to boil and lower to a simmer for 10 minutes. Remove the chouriço and remove from casings and shred or chop into small to medium pieces and leave aside. NOTE* Do not get rid of the water used to boil the chouriço, please leave aside.

Heat milk or broth until almost at a boil and pour over the bread. Using your hands or a fork mix together and leave aside, letting the bread completely absorb the liquid. Once that's absorbed, add about half of the liquid of the water used to boil the chouriço and let the bread absorb that completely.

In a separate bowl mix and beat together the eggs, shredded chouriço, red pepper sauce, paprika, chopped parsley, salt and pepper to taste and pour over the bread. Using your hands mix everything together and leave aside. It's up to you how chucking you leave your bread... The more you mix the more the bread will breakdown into smaller pieces.

In a large frying pan, sauté the chopped onion, garlic in olive oil. season with a little salt and cook until onion is translucent and almost caramelized.

Add the bread mixture into the pan and stir together. You want to make sure the egg is well incorporated. At this point you can place the mixture into a buttered baking dish and bake in a 350° F oven, uncovered for 30 minutes. If you like your stuffing a little drier you can bake for another 10 minutes.

Enjoy!!!

my sister isabel's stewed chicken and potatoes

Receita de minha irma Isabel de Galinha Guisada om Batatas

My sister Isabel will be the first to tell you that cooking is not her favorite thing. She does it because she has to sometimes, but would be happy going to a restaurant everyday if she could. That said, there are a few dishes she knows how to do and do very well; this dish is one of them. It was always a hit with her children and to this day she will make it for them for their special occasion family dinners. When I got married she was very eager to share the recipe with me. Yes, my mom would make it too, but my sister's dish actually was better then my mom's because its gravy was definitely more lemony and creamy. It's a very easy and quick dinner to make which is important when you're trying to make dinner and only have 45 minutes to spare. Don't be fooled: the taste will make it look like you have worked so hard over the stove.

Ingredients:
1 whole chicken, cut in parts
4-5 large potatoes, roughly cut in cubes
2 large onions, chopped
2 cloves of garlic, minced
1-2 tablespoons of hot chopped peppers
2 tablespoons of paprika
Salt and pepper to taste
4-5 egg yolks
Juice of 1 lemon
Oil
Hot water

Directions:
Cover the bottom of a large dutch oven pan with oil and over medium heat sauté the onions until they are translucent in color. Add the chicken parts, then season with salt, pepper, paprika, hot chopped peppers, and garlic. Sauté everything together for about 10 minutes. You need to make sure the chicken is well covered in the paprika and if needed you can add another tablespoon to the pan.

Add the potatoes and stir and sauté for another minute. Then add enough hot water to cover both the chicken and potatoes. (Don't add cold water; that will make the cooking stop and will take longer to cook.) Cover the pan and simmer for 20 minutes or until the chicken is cooked.

In a seperate bowl, beat together the egg yolks and lemon juice and leave aside. Once the chicken is cooked, spoon out the broth and add a little at a time to the bowl with egg and lemon and mix together. Next, pour the mixture back into the pan and stir well. Remove from the heat and cover. By doing it this way the egg will not cook, but instead will thicken the broth to a creamy lemon perfection!

stewed chicken with rice

Galinha Guisada com Arroz

Even though my mom would make this dish almost every week, it was my sister Isabel who taught me how to make it. She also loves this dish and would often make it for her family as well. It's another very easy and simple dish to make during the week. There are some variations and some people like to add linguiça to it. Even though I have tried it with the added sausage, I prefer the traditional way to make it. But you can test it both ways and see what you like best.

Ingredients:

1 lb of chicken thighs (4 pieces)
1 onion, chopped fine
1 garlic clove, minced
1 tablespoon of paprika
1 teaspoon of cinnamon
1 tablespoon of crushed red hot peppers (more or less depending how spicy you like it)
Salt and pepper to taste
Olive oil, 2-4 tablespoons
1 cup of rice

Directions:

In a large deep skillet over medium heat add the olive oil and sauté the onions and garlic. Add the chicken thighs and add the paprika, cinnamon, crushed red hot peppers and some salt and pepper to taste. Mix everything together and make sure that the chicken is covered with all the seasonings. Add 3 to 4 cups of water, making sure that it covers the chicken and bring it to a boil for 15-20 minutes. Last, add 1 cup of rice and simmer for 20 minutes or until the rice is cooked.

steak with an egg on horseback

Bife Com Um ovo a Cavalo

Ingredients:

4 sirloin steaks, ½ inch thick
8 sliced garlic cloves (thinly sliced)
Salt and pepper to taste
2 cups red wine
1 bay leaf
1 tablespoon of crushed red peppers
2 tablespoons butter
2 tablespoons olive oil
½ cup heavy cream
4 eggs
1 pickled roasted red pepper strip (optional)

Directions:

In a large deep container, place your steaks and add the garlic slices, salt, pepper, wine and crushed red peppers. Make sure that the steaks are covered in all the marinade. Cover the container and leave in the refrigerator at for least for 3 hours, but it is always best to marinate overnight. (The steaks will be much more flavorful if you do.)

In a large skillet over medium-high heat, heat the butter and oil. Reserving the marinade remove the steaks. Place them in skillet and fry the steaks 3 minutes on each side. Remove them to a clean plate and cover to keep warm.

Add the reserved marinade to the hot skillet and deglaze the browned bits at the bottom of the pan. Remove from heat and quickly whisk in the cream. Place over medium-low heat and return the steaks to the pan and cook about three minutes. The sauce will thicken a little.

In a separate skillet, fry the eggs while the steaks are still cooking.

When you're ready to serve have your steak on the plate with the fried egg placed on top of it and a strip of the red hot pepper on the very top. Pour some sauce around the steak and serve with fried potatoes and/or vegetables.

Desserts

sweet rice/rice pudding

Arroz Doce

As far as I can remember, rice pudding has always been one of my favorite desserts. When I was growing up my mom would make our favorite meal and dessert for each of our birthdays and I would always request rice pudding for my dessert. I could have cake another time, but rice pudding was special and it still is to this day. What I also like is that my children love it as much as I do and while I'm mastering the rice pudding recipe, they are all so eager to help scrape the pan after I finish making a batch. It brings back great memories of me sneaking in the kitchen and trying to do the same.

Over the years I have come across so many rice pudding recipes that are very tasty, but the three recipes I will share with you are from my Mom, my Aunt Lilia and cousin Laureana. All are slightly different in consistencies: my mom's recipe is a thick consistency that you could cut with a knife and pick it up to eat it if you want. My Aunt Lilia's is by far the creamiest and Laureana's recipe is in between the two. All three recipes will yield two large serving dishes of the rice pudding. On several occasions I have cut each recipe in half when it's just my immediate family that I'm serving or we are just looking for a quick fix with no leftovers.

My Mom's Recipe

Ingredients:

2 cups of long grain white rice (I use River Rice)
2 cups of very hot water
4 cups of very hot milk
2 cups of sugar
Peel of 1 lemon
$^{1}/_{8}$ teaspoon of salt
6 egg yolks
Cinnamon to decorate

Directions:

Have your rice rinsed and soaking in water for about an hour before you begin making the pudding. In a medium saucepan, bring the soaked rice and hot water to a boil. Lower the heat, cover and continue to simmer until all the water has been completely absorbed.

In the meantime, in a separate small saucepan bring the milk to an almost boil and pour into the rice. Add the lemon peels and bring everything to a boil again, stirring constantly until the rice has absorbed all the milk.

Then add the sugar and again constantly stir for about another 30 minutes until the rice has thickened to a point that if you take your spoon, you can separate the rice long enough to see the bottom of the pan. At this time you can taste the rice and see if it has cooked. If it hasn't cooked you will need to add another cup of very hot water to it and stir again until this water has been completely absorbed again.

Once the rice is cooked, whisk together the egg yolks in a separate bowl and mix in a couple of spoonfuls of the rice to it, then incorporate it back in the rice pan and cook for another 5-10 minutes.

It is very important to not just add the egg yolks into the pan of cooked rice. If you do you'll get scrambled eggs. You need to make sure the yolks get cooked, but adding the rice to the bowl one spoonful at a time gives the eggs time to adjust to the heat before adding the whole mixture back into the rice.

The last step is to pour the rice on to large serving dishes, making sure to remove all the lemon peels before decorating with cinnamon on top. Some people like to create lines or designs with the cinnamon; personally I just like to sprinkle it on.

My Aunt Lilia's Recipe

Ingredients:
2 cups of white rice, preferably the River Rice brand
2 cups of sugar
2 cups of water
6 cups of whole milk
4 tablespoons (½ stick) of salted butter
Peel from 2 to 3 lemons
10 egg yolks
Cinnamon to decorate

Directions:
Have your rice rinsed and soaking in water for about an hour before you begin making the pudding. In a medium sauce pan, bring to a boil the water, rice, butter and lemon peels. Then, lower the heat and continue to simmer until all the water has been completely absorbed, making sure to stir occasionally so that the rice does not stick to the pan. Afterwards, remove the lemon peels.

In a separate medium sauce pan, heat the milk until almost at a boil. Pour milk into rice, add the sugar and stir everything together and bring to a boil again. Next, lower the heat and constantly stir until the rice has absorbed all the liquid. This takes about 30 to 45 minutes or until the rice has thickened to the point that if you take your spoon you can separate the rice long enough to see the bottom of the pan. At this time you will need to sample the rice and see if it has cooked. If it hasn't you will need to add another cup of very hot milk to it and keep stirring again until it has been completely absorbed.

In a different bowl you'll need to separate your eggs, since you will only be using the egg yolks. Beat the egg yolks, and once the rice is cooked you will add a couple of heaping spoonfuls of the hot rice to the egg yolks, one spoonful at a time. Then you will incorporate the egg mixture back into the rice pan and cook for another 5-10 minutes.

The last step is to pour rice pudding in serving dishes and decorate with cinnamon.

My cousin Laureana's Recipe

Ingredients:
2 cups of extra long grain rice (preferably the Carolina brand)
2 cups of hot water
2 cups of sugar
4 cups of warm whole milk
Peel of 2 lemons
Dash of salt
1 teaspoon of vanilla if desired
3 egg yolks
Cinnamon to decorate

Directions:
Have your rice rinsed and soaking in water for about an hour before you begin making the pudding.

In a medium saucepan, place the rice, water, salt and lemon peels. Stir everything together and bring to a boil. Cover and reduce heat to a simmer and continue until all the water has been absorbed.

Next, add the warm milk to the rice mixture and once again bring everything to a boil. Continually stir the rice and reduce the heat to a high simmer until the rice is cooked.

Add the sugar and vanilla and continue to stir until you can take your spoon and separate the rice long enough to see the bottom of the pan. My cousin called it "seeing the road". Once you see "the road" your next step is to incorporate the egg yolks into the rice mixture using the following steps.

Separate your eggs and in a clean bowl, beat the egg yolks really well. Then you're going to add the rice to this bowl one tablespoon at a time, until the egg is well mixed in. Now add the egg mixture back into the pan with rice and cook for another 5-10 minutes.

Pour the rice pudding onto large serving dishes and/or individual serving dishes. Make sure to remove lemon peels before serving and decorate with cinnamon.

fried dough

Malassadas

Growing up my mom would make malassadas just for special occasions. They would especially be made for what we call today Fat Tuesday, the day before Ash Wednesday. Her malassadas would be light and airy with a hint of lemon. She would sometimes not stretch the dough but instead make little balls of dough, which was like our version of donut holes. I remember eating them as quickly as they were being made. Since I never found my mom's recipe I have two slightly different versions, one from my Aunt Lilia and one from my Aunt Inez. I think both are very close to my mom's recipe. The ingredients and the dough are slightly different but both follow the same direction on how to fry. I hope you enjoy them as much as my family and I do because both are really delicious. Try and make both recipes, and then you can decide which one is your own favorite!

My Aunt Lilia's Version

Ingredients:

3 cups of all-purpose flour
½ teaspoon of salt
7 large eggs at room temperature
½ cup (1 stick) of butter, melted
¼ cup of sugar
2 envelopes of active yeast, ¼ oz in each envelope
¼ cup of lukewarm water to dissolve the yeast
Zest of 2 lemons
Milk as needed for dipping hands
3 cups of oil for frying
3 cups of sugar for dredging

Mixing Directions:

In a small bowl dissolve the yeast packets with the ¼ cup of lukewarm water and leave aside.

In a small saucepan melt the stick of butter and leave aside.

In a large bowl beat together the eggs, sugar, butter and lemon zest until creamy. Then add in small intervals the flour and salt and continue to mix well. Lastly, you will add the dissolved yeast into the mix and blend well. Knead the dough by hand until everything is well incorporated. On the few occasions that I have made this recipe, the batter was a little on the wet side and I did have to add a few tablespoons of flour to the mix during the final kneading.

Cover the large bowl with some kitchen towels and place the bowl in a warm place, free of drafts, and wait till the dough doubles in size. This can take an hour or two depending on the weather. If it's a cold day expect it to take a little longer. My Aunt Lilia suggested that I turn the oven on in the kitchen and have the bowl of dough near by. The extra heat will help in those extra cold days to make it rise faster.

My Aunt Ines's Version

Ingredients:

2 envelopes of active yeast, ¼ oz in each envelope
¼ cup of lukewarm milk to dissolve the yeast
4 cups of all-purpose flour
1 teaspoon of salt
¼ cup of sugar
4 eggs, beaten
½ cup of oil or melted butter
1 shot glass of whiskey or brandy
⅓ cup of warm milk
Zest of 1 lemon
Milk as needed for dipping hands
3 cups of oil for frying
3 cups of sugar for dredging

Mixing Directions:

In a small bowl dissolve the yeast packets with the ¼ cup of lukewarm milk and leave aside.

In a small saucepan melt butter and leave aside.

In a large bowl add the flour and form a well in the bowl by pushing the flour to the sides of the bowl. Then you will add to the center of the well the beaten eggs, salt, lemon zest, sugar, milk, melted butter, a shot of whiskey and the yeast. Using a wooden spoon begin to combine everything together. When it becomes too hard to mix with the spoon, use your hands to mix then knead the dough well together. At this point, if the dough is too dry you can add a tablespoon of milk, or if it's too wet you can add a tablespoon of flour. Continue until everything is well incorporated. Cover the bowl with some kitchen towels and place the bowl in a warm spot with no drafts and wait until the dough doubles in size.

This can take an hour or two depending on the weather, but this recipe has a shot of alcohol in it to help the yeast rise faster. My aunt said that the brandy or whiskey gives the yeast the heat it needs to help it rise, especially in cold weather. I was worried the first time I made it that we would be able to taste the whiskey in the finished product. But to my surprise there was no whiskey taste.

Directions for frying both dough recipes:
Once the dough rises and doubles in size, you are now ready to fry the dough. In a large, deep pot such as a dutch oven, heat the 3 cups of oil over low heat. Using a small bowl of milk to dip your hands, take about 1 tablespoon of dough in your hand. The dough is on the sticky side so make sure you have enough milk on your hands to stretch out the dough until it is round and thin. Then drop it into the oil very gently, making sure to turn them on both sides until they are a golden brown.

It's very important to make sure that the oil does not get too hot. What will happen is that the outside of the malassadas will fry up quickly and also begin to burn but the inside will stay raw and undercooked. So be very careful and keep a close eye.

As soon as they are done frying I always place them first on a tray lined with paper towels so that any excess oil can be absorbed. Then I have another deep-sided tray filled with sugar ready, and while the malassadas are still warm, dredge them through the sugar; you can also sprinkle some cinnamon if you like. Also, if you can get extra helping hands it would be a lot easier, too. I remember my sister stretching the dough, my mom frying and my other sister and I putting sugar over them: great memories which I will never forget.

Now you have made your batch of malassadas...never again will you be able to eat that greasy kind you find sometimes being sold on weekends only! This is as good as it gets!!

sugar coated peanuts

Amendoins Cobertos de Açucar

What could be better than peanuts covered in sugar? This recipe is one my family's favorite, especially around the holidays or special occasions. The recipe can also be substituted with any nut of your choice; almonds are our second favorite!

Ingredients:
4 cups of unsalted Spanish Peanuts (keeping the red skin on)
2 cups of granulated sugar
1 cup of water

Directions:
Dissolve sugar in water in a heavy duty saucepan over medium heat. Add the peanuts and cook until there is no syrup and all sugar is on the peanuts in a crystallized way.

Transfer the peanuts onto a foil-lined baking sheet and spread the peanuts, making sure that the peanuts don't stick together.

Place tray in 300° F oven and bake for 30 minutes to allow the coating to dry and become crunchy. Keep stirring the peanuts around every ten minutes so that they bake evenly.

Remove the peanuts from the oven and let them cool off. Once cool you can break apart some of the peanuts that have stuck together and enjoy each crunchy bite.

portuguese popovers

Cavacas

These light pastry popovers are covered with a sugar glaze and are usually made around the season of Carnivale. Because this was my mother's favorite treat, my family usually had it at every special occasion. Some people make them bite sized, but I like them best in the larger size and smothered in sugar glaze with lemon zest.

Makes 24

Ingredients:
2 cups of flour
1 cup of oil
½ cup of whole milk
8 eggs at room temperature

Directions:
Preheat oven to 350° F.

Grease regular-sized muffin tins or popover tins. Using an electric mixer beat all ingredients for at least 20 minutes without stopping. I highly recommend using a stand mixer on this recipe with the mixer set on level 6. Fill the muffin or popover tins no more than half way.

Bake on the middle rack of the oven. For moist cavacas, bake for about 45 minutes; if you like them on the dry side, bake for 1 hour. They will get to a nice golden color and you can "popover" the pans when they're done.

Sugar Glaze:
2 cups of confectioner's sugar
Zest of one lemon
2 tablespoons of milk (more or less depending on the thickness you like)

While they are still warm, spoon the glaze over each one or just submerge each one in the glaze. Either way you can't go wrong. Serve on the same day, since it will dry even more for the following day.

milk tarts

Queijadas de Leite

This recipe has always been a staple at almost every family event I have ever attended when I was growing up. I had forgotten just how easy it was to make, until my cousin Helena reminded me of the recipe. Since then it has once again become a staple at my parties.

This recipe makes about 3 dozen tarts.

Ingredients:
4 extra large eggs or 5 large eggs
3 cups of granulated sugar
1 ½ cups of all purpose flour
3 cups milk
1 cup (2 sticks) of butter (soften at room temp)
1 lemon, peeled
1 teaspoon of pure vanilla* optional
Confectioners sugar, for dusting* optional

Directions:
Preheat oven at 350° F.

Grease cupcake pans. Since the tarts tend to caramelize and stick when baked, it's best to make sure you grease the pans real well. Then leave aside.

Using a small saucepan over medium heat, add the milk and lemon peels and bring to a slow simmer. Remove from heat and let the milk become infused with the lemon flavor. Don't forget to remove the peels before you use the milk in the recipe.

In a large bowl, add the eggs and sugar and beat until a creamy consistency. Then add the softened butter, then add the flour a little at a time. Add the lemon-infused milk as well as vanilla and beat everything well together. This batter has a different texture, unlike a cake batter, it's very runny. So resist the urge to add more flour. Once everything is well mixed fill tins about 3/4 of the way. Place in preheated oven and bake for 40-45 minutes, depending on your oven or until tops are nice and golden color.

The tarts will be a creamy but firm texture on the inside, and lightly crisp and caramelized on the outside. Even though you'll be tempted to eat them right away, make sure to wait till they are cooled off completely before you bite into them.

Before you serve, dust them with confectioners sugar.

custard tarts

Tigeladas

My mom only made these egg tarts for very special occasions. They are very close to an individual flan, but the consistency is a little denser and you don't have to worry about making caramel. The lemon infused milk in this recipe gives this tart an amazing flavor. It will have you wondering why you've never tasted it before!!

This recipe makes 8 small tarts, but the recipe can be easily doubled.
If you don't have tart pans you can substitute by using the jumbo muffin pans.

Ingredients:
5 extra large eggs
¼ cup of granulated sugar
2 cups of whole milk
Peel of 1 to 2 lemons depending on size
1 teaspoon of cinnamon
1 tablespoon of flour

Directions:
Preheat oven at 350° F. Grease the little tart pans and leave aside.

Using a saucepan over medium heat, add the milk and lemon peel and bring to a slow simmer for about 5 minutes. Remove from heat and let it cool down.

In a large bowl beat together the eggs and sugar. Mix in the flour and cinnamon. Remove the lemon peels from the milk before adding the milk to the bowl and beating everything together. Let stand and rest for about 10 minutes, then pour into tart pans and bake for 1 hour.

When you serve the tigelalads, make sure to dust it with powdered sugar. Everyone will be impressed!

sighs/meringue

Suspiros

These sweet meringue treats say it all—once you try them, you'll sigh with enjoyment! This recipe is one of the easiest to make and stops any sweet-tooth craving in its track.

Ingredients:
3 egg whites
1 cup granulated sugar
Zest of one lemon

Directions:
Preheat oven to 325° F and line 2 cookie sheets with parchment paper.

In a large glass or metal bowl, whip together all ingredients until stiff peaks form. (It takes me about 7 minutes to get to that point.) A good test to know you're at that point is to spoon out the meringue and hold the spoon upside down; if the meringue is thick enough, it should stay on the spoon.

Scoop the meringue by the tablespoon onto the parchment-lined cookie sheets and bake for 15 minutes, or until the meringue is a light golden color. Let them cool completely.

What you will find once you take a bite is that under this crispy shell is a soft center that just melts in your mouth. I hope you try these tasty treats soon.

marble cake

Bolo de Mármore

I have two recipes for marble cake. The first came from my Aunt Lilia who would always have some homemade cake waiting for us when we went to visit her family. I remember my aunt telling us that it was extra tasty when it was served with a glass of Port or Madeira wine. It was a memorable experience having it with some wine, and one I still enjoy. The cake is light and buttery and makes a wonderful combination with the wine.

The other recipe is from my sister Isabel. As far as I can remember, my sister would make this cake for every special occasion. We just knew if she said she was bringing a dessert, she would be bringing her special cake. She would call it Bolo de Piquenique / Picnic Cake and tell us the most important ingredient was love: if you weren't in the greatest mood the cake would not come out well. Only recently did she share this recipe with me and finally admitted that she made up the name! It is a marble cake, a very delicious one at that. She thought that by giving it a special name, it would be extra special! And she was right, it might be a marble cake, but to our family it will always be the delicious Bolo de Piquenique!

My Aunt Lilia's recipe

Ingredients:

1 heaping cup of sugar
2 sticks (1 cup) and 2 tablespoons of softened butter
4 eggs at room temperature
2 teaspoons of vanilla
1 heaping cup of flour
2 teaspoons of baking powder
¼ teaspoon of salt
1 tablespoon of whole milk
4 tablespoons of cocoa powder

Directions:

Preheat oven at 350° F. Grease and flour a large bundt or tube pan and leave aside.

In a small bowl sift together the flour, baking powder and salt and leave aside.

In a separate large bowl cream together the sugar and butter using a hand mixer. Add the eggs one at a time and lastly add the vanilla. Make sure everything is well beaten together. Slowly start adding in the flour mixture into this bowl and continue to beat everything together at a high speed. Finally you will beat in the milk, especially if the batter has become a little dry. (On a few occasions I have not added the milk, since I felt the batter was wet enough and didn't need it.) Divide the batter in half and keep one bowl vanilla; in the second bowl add the cocoa powder and mix well.

Take your greased and floured pan and add to it one large spoonful of batter at a time, alternating between vanilla and chocolate. Using a knife, swirl the two flavors together.

Place in preheated oven and let bake for 35-40 minutes or until a wooden skewer inserted inside comes out clean.

My Sister Isabel's Recipe

Ingredients:

2 heaping cups of sugar
2 sticks (1 cup) of butter at room temperature
4 eggs at room temperature
1 cup of whole milk
3 heaping cups of flour
1 tablespoon of baking powder
1 teaspoon of salt
Zest of 1 lemon
2 tablespoons of cocoa powder

Directions:

Preheat oven at 350° F. Grease and flour a large bundt or tube pan and leave aside.

In a large bowl sift together the flour, baking powder, and salt, then leave aside.

Separate the egg whites from the yolks into two separate bowls. Beat the egg whites until they are firm and form high peaks; leave aside.

In a large bowl using a hand mixer, beat the butter, sugar and egg yolks. After beating everything together really well, add the milk then slowly add the flour. Mix in the lemon zest and once everything is well incorporated you can add the egg whites and fold them into the batter and mix well.

In a separate bowl, spoon out 4 tablespoons of the batter and mix together with the cocoa.

Pour half the batter into greased pan, then spoon the cocoa batter mixture on top and then pour the other half of batter on top. With a knife, swirl through all three layers of the batter to form the marble design. Place in preheated oven and lower the heat to 300° F and let bake for 60 minutes or until an inserted wooden skewer in the cake comes out clean. When you remove the cake from the oven, cover the cake with a dish towel and let it rest for another 30 minutes before you remove it from the pan.

biscuits made with cream

Biscoitos de Nata

Makes 4 dozen biscuits.

Ingredients:
8 cups of flour
1 pint of heavy cream
2 cups of sugar
4 large eggs
2 teaspoons of baking powder
1 ½ cups (3 sticks) of butter (at room temperature)
1 tablespoon of lard (at room temperature)
1 teaspoon of salt
Zest of 1 lemon

Directions:
Preheat oven at 350° F, and lightly grease baking trays.

In an extra large bowl combine the flour, baking powder and salt. Mix well and leave aside.

In a separate large bowl using a hand mixer, cream together the 3 sticks of butter and lard. Mix in the sugar and eggs and beat together at a high speed until creamy. Then add the heavy cream and beat for another 2 minutes. Once everything is well incorporated, mix in the lemon zest and leave aside.

Make a well in the bottom of the bowl of flour by pushing the flour to the sides of the bowl. Then, you're going to slowly pour the creamy mixture into the well. Using a mixing spoon, start blending them together until the dough gets too hard and then you will need to knead the rest by hand. Take the dough out of the bowl and place onto a floured surface and continue to knead until you can form the dough into a large ball.

Now you can start and break off small pieces of dough and roll them out into small size balls or into shapes. Most of the time my mom would roll out a small piece of the dough and form almost a wreath shape with the ends crisscrossing each other.

These biscuits are so yummy that we really didn't care what shape they were in. I know you'll agree too once you try one!

Place the shaped dough on the baking trays and bake them until they are a golden color. Depending on your oven it should take about 15-20 minutes. The one thing you don't want to do is over bake. If you do, the biscuits will be very dry.

rosettes of egypt

Rosas do Egipto

I remember my mom making these for special occasions and how we would each wait our turn to have one. She would be so careful as not to burn them and prepare them just so and we would wait till one wasn't perfect. Those not so perfect would go in a separate dish for the family to eat and the best would go on the special tray to bring to a party. We were always hoping for those not so perfect; they were still warm, crispy and sweet. When I made them for the first time I burned a few, and then some didn't come out of the form that well until I got the hang of it. They were not perfect by any means, but they were delicious!

Makes 6 dozen

Ingredients:

2 eggs
2 tablespoons of sugar
1 cup of milk
1 cup of all purpose flour
½ teaspoon of salt
Oil for frying

Directions:

Beat 2 eggs slightly. Add 2 tablespoons sugar, then add the cup milk. Sift one cup of all-purpose flour and 1/2 teaspoon salt; stir into the egg mixture and beat until smooth (should be about the consistency of heavy cream).

In a 5-quart deep fryer fill it about 2/3 full with cooking oil and heat to 400° F. Dip rosette form into the hot oil to heat it; drain excess oil on paper towels. Dip heated form into the batter not more than ¾ their depth. If only a thin layer of batter adheres to the forms, dip them again until a smooth layer adheres. Plunge batter-coated form into hot oil and cook until active bubble ceases. This does not take very long and you have to keep an eye on it or else it can burn very quickly. With fork, ease rosettes off form and onto paper towels to drain. While still warm, dip into confectioners' sugar or sift sugar over them.

golden slices

Fatias Douradas

I love this dessert. My mom would make this special treat when we had some day-old bread. It is very similar to French toast, but instead of grilling the bread this is deep fried! Then they get covered in lots of sugar and sometimes a little bit of cinnamon. Even to this day, I use this recipe as a quick go-to dessert for surprise visitors as well a cure for a quick sweet tooth attack for any family member. My daughters have even raised it to another level and now add a scoop of ice cream on top of it too! It is truly a delicious treat for everyone to enjoy.

Besides day old bread, sometimes my mom would also make them with some day-old sweet-bread that had become too dry. But since we usually ate the sweetbread faster then she could make it. It wasn't that often that we would have them that way.

Ingredients:

Day-old bread, sliced thick
3-5 eggs (depending on how much bread you have)
1 cup of milk (depending again on how much bread you can adjust)
A dash of salt
Oil for frying
Granulated sugar
Cinnamon

In a shallow baking dish beat the eggs, milk and salt together and leave aside. In a very heavy skillet add oil to the cold pan, leaving at least two inches of space at the top of the pan. Begin heating the oil over medium-high heat.

Carefully soak the slices in the egg and milk mixture before adding them into the skillet, leaving lots of space around each piece so the slices will cook evenly.

Watch carefully as they cook, regulating the heat if necessary. When the slices start to get a nice golden color, it's done. Remove them with a slotted spoon and drop them onto paper towels to drain.

Then you can cover them or sprinkle them with sugar and cinnamon and enjoy each bite!

pineapple

Ananás

In my opinion the best and sweetest pineapple is only available in Sao Miguel. With so many pineapple plantations, or as we call them estufas de ananás, throughout the island, you can't help but notice all the white-chalk windowed hothouses almost everywhere you look.

At almost every meal, pineapple can be the accompaniment or the main dish. It could be pineapple jam in the morning, fresh cut slices with lunch, pineapple cake or tart for a mid-afternoon treat or an evening dessert, and last but not least, pineapple liquor for the end of the day.

Every home that I visited had fresh pineapple available, and I never said no when I was offered. Everyone would tell me that eating fresh pineapple after each meal helps you digest your food. I don't know if that's a proven fact, but I won't argue it. The pineapple shape in Sao Miguel is smaller and rounder than what I am accustomed to. But that small size packs a lot of flavor and you will encounter the sweetest smell and taste you've ever experienced before.

I am also very lucky that my cousin Ricardo's wife Cristina is from a family that owns one of Sao Miguel's pineapple plantations. Her parents, Mr. and Mrs. José & Filomena Soares, were very generous with their time and gave me a tour, explaining to me the steps it takes to cultivate pineapples. Mr. Soares shared that even though they are harvested year round, there is a difference between those picked in the winter and summer months. The winter crop tends to be sweet and sour, so these pineapples will be used mostly for jams and liquors. Sometimes they are grilled and served along with one of my favorites: fried blood sausage, aka morcela. But the summer crop is the sweeter of the two seasons and is enjoyed by everyone, whether fresh or baked, in so many desserts. I happened to visit during the summer months, so I guess I need to make another visit, but this time in the winter...just to compare of course!

Helpful hints for buying and preparing your next fresh pineapple:

How to pick your pineapple:

When choosing a fresh ripe pineapple, make sure it has firm, golden to brown skin (not too green). A ripe pineapple will also have a strong, fresh pineapple smell.

How to cut your fresh pineapple:

Cut off the leaves and about a half inch of the top and bottom of the fruit. Turn the pineapple upright onto its base. To peel the pineapple you will need a long knife, which will make it easier for you to follow the contour of the pineapple. Once you have completely peeled the pineapple, check the fruit over for any skin or "eyes" you may have missed. Remove any remaining "eyes" with a paring knife. To slice the pineapple into rings, remove the core with a pineapple corer and slice to desired thickness.

pineapple upside down cake

Bolo de Ananás

Pineapple Upside Down Cake is probably one of those cakes everyone has had at least once in their life. The difference with this recipe is that you don't use canned pineapple. Instead you use fresh pineapple, preferably pineapple from the Azores if you're really lucky!

Ingredients for Caramel:
1 cup of granulated sugar
2 teaspoons of water

Ingredients for Cake:
1 ¼ cup of granulated sugar
4 large eggs, separated
1 cup (2 sticks) of salted butter, softened
1 ¾ cups of all purpose flour
1 teaspoon of baking powder
1 fresh pineapple, peeled, cored and cut into slices

Directions:
Preheat oven at 350° F. Grease a 9-inch round cake pan with butter and sprinkle some flour to cover the pan. Make sure to tap out any excess flour that doesn't stick to the butter and leave pan aside.

Prepare the caramel by using a small saucepan (preferably a non-stick) over medium heat; add the sugar and few teaspoons of water. The sugar will begin to melt and slowly the color will go to golden caramel. Once at that stage, remove the pan from the heat since it can quickly burn the caramel if left on too long. Now you can pour the caramel into the bottom of the pan. Quickly turn the pan and tilt so that the caramel can cover as much of the pan as possible.
**Don't worry if you have a small spot empty and the caramel has completely hardened. I find that once the pan goes in the oven the heat will melt the caramel again, and it seems to cover those empty spots*

Place the fresh pineapple slices on top of the caramel at the bottom of the pan. Leave aside.
**I was able to use 7 slices of pineapple. I placed one in the center and six surrounding. But you can do what ever design you would like.*

In a medium bowl mix together the flour with the baking powder and leave aside.

In a separate medium bowl beat the egg whites until they are firm and form high peaks and leave aside.

In a large bowl beat together the sugar and butter until creamy. Add the egg yolks and continue to mix, then add in small intervals the flour mixture and continue to mix well together. Then using a spatula or wooden spoon gently mix in the egg whites, being very careful not to over mix.

Pour the mixture into the prepared cake pan and bake for 45-50 minutes, or until the cake is a golden brown color. You can also check if the cake is done by inserting a toothpick or a very sharp blade, which should come out clean. Remove the cake from the oven and let it cool before you transfer the cake on to a serving dish.

Once the cake has cooled, make sure to use a sharp knife between the cake and the pan and loosen the cake from the pan. Take the serving dish and place over the cake pan and flip over. Your Upside Down Cake should come out of the pan onto the dish. You can serve the cake warm or let it cool down to room temperature.

regional pineapple pie

Torta de Ananás Regional

Dough:
2 cups of all-purpose flour
1 large egg, beaten
3 to 4 tablespoons milk
4 tablespoons (½ stick) of butter, softened

Filling:
1 whole pineapple at least 1 lb in size, chopped into small pieces
¾ cup of sugar, more or less depending if pineapple isn't sweet enough
4 large eggs, beaten
4 tablespoons (½ stick) of butter
1 tablespoon cornstarch
¼ cup of milk

Directions:
Preheat oven at 350° F. Grease 12-inch tart pan and leave aside.

In a large bowl, add 2 cups of flour and form a well, by pushing the flour to the sides of the bowl. Add the beaten egg, milk and softened butter to the center well. Using your hands slowly incorporate the dry flour into the wet egg mixture. Keep mixing and kneading by hand until a round ball is formed. If the dough is wet, add a few tablespoons of flour; if too dry add a tablespoon at a time of milk. Place dough on a floured surface and roll out the dough, until it's large enough to fit over the tart pan. Place the dough into tart pan, making sure it fits into each indentation of the pan. Leave aside.

To make the filling, in a large saucepan set over low heat, add the 4 beaten eggs with butter and sugar. Keep whipping with a spoon or hand mixer until creamy, then add the chopped pineapple. In a separate bowl, dissolve the cornstarch with the milk, then add into saucepan and stir constantly until thickened.

Pour the pineapple mixture into the tart pan and bake in oven for 60 minutes or until golden. Let it cool before serving.

velvet pudding aka flan

Pudim de Veludo

This wonderful recipe, called velvet pudding, is also called milk or caramel pudding. I didn't realize that every time someone was offering me some pudding they were actually offering me what I always thought was called flan. Well I was wrong! I was quickly told the Spanish call it flan, but we call it pudding (as we would say "pudim"). So, now I stand corrected to never to make that mistake again. Well, at least I'll try my best. This recipe was given to me by my cousin Helena. She served it to me and it was lighter than the usual "Pudim" I have tried before. Since then I have made it several times for my family and each time seems to be better than the last. I hope you agree.

Ingredients:
4 cups of whole milk
One lb of granulated sugar
8 eggs
Zest of one lemon
2 teaspoons of vanilla
6 tablespoons of sugar for the caramel

Directions:
Preheat the oven at 350° F.

Using a medium non-stick saucepan add 6 tablespoons of sugar and heat the sugar until it liquifies and then caramelizes. Once it does, pour the caramel into an 8-inch tube cake pan and quickly line the bottom of the pan before the caramel begins to harden. Once the caramel hardens, you will not be able to spread the caramel any further.

In a large bowl beat the eggs and sugar together until creamy. Add the lemon zest with the vanilla, and finally the milk. Beat everything together and pour the mixture into the prepared pan lined with caramel.

Place the cake pan into another larger roasting pan and add at least 2 inches of boiling water into the roasting pan. You need to be very careful not to add any water into the pan with the egg mixture. This baking technique is called banho-maria or bain-marie water bath. It's important not to skip this step since the water provides an even distribution of heat for the pudding to bake properly.

Insert the pans into oven and bake for 1 hour.

Insert a sharp knife into the pudding and if it comes out clean it is done.

Remove the cake pan from the roasting pan, and let the cake pan cool and then refrigerate overnight for best results.

To serve, place a deep plate on top of cake pan and flip the pan over. The caramel sauce will be liquified and cover the velvet pudding…simply delicious!!

Here are some variations you can use when making your pudim. It's very simple to add different flavors into the same recipe; the key is infusing flavor into the milk.

- Instead of using the zest, you can infuse the milk with several strips of orange or lemon peels over medium-low heat for several minutes. Just make sure to let the milk cool off and remove the peels before using.

- You can also make a very traditional green tea pudim by using 2-3 tablespoons of our very own Gorreana green tea in loose leaf. All you need to do is combine the milk and tea leaves in a small saucepan and bring to a simmer over medium-low heat. Remove the pan from heat and allow the milk to steep for about 10 minutes. Strain the mixture into a bowl, discard the tea leaves, and let the milk cool before using.

caramel pudding aka flan

Pudim de Caramelo

This recipe came from my Aunt Lilia. She would always serve this for the open house parties she would have around Christmas. It's really creamy and delicious and perfect for any occasion.

Ingredients:

12 eggs
12 tablespoons of sugar
1 teaspoon lemon zest
½ teaspoon of salt
1 ½ cups of heavy cream
6 ½ cups of whole milk

Directions:

Preheat the oven at 350° F.

Using a medium non-stick saucepan add 6 tablespoons of sugar and heat the sugar until it liquifies and then caramelizes. Once it does, pour the caramel into a 10-inch tube cake pan and quickly line the bottom of the pan, before the caramel begins to harden. Once the caramel hardens, you will not be able to spread the caramel any further.

In a large bowl beat the eggs with sugar, lemon zest and salt. Add the cream and milk.

Pour the egg mixture into the prepared pan with caramel and then place that cake pan into a larger roasting pan with at least 2 inches of hot water added to the bottom. You need to be very careful not to add any water into the pan that holds the egg mixture.

Insert in oven and bake for 1 hour. Insert a sharp knife into the pudding and if it comes out clean it is done.

Remove the cake pan from the roasting pan, and let the cake pan cool and then refrigerate overnight.

To serve, place a dish with sides to go over cake pan and flip the pan over. The caramel sauce will be liquified again, so be careful not to spill any of it! Enjoy!

coconut lemon cake

Bolo de Coco e Limão

This recipe is one of my favorites. The first time I had this cake was at my niece Emma's birthday party. Her great-aunt Fatima Duarte baked it for her, and I am so glad she did. I am also glad that she shared this recipe with me and now everyone can also enjoy it. It's moist and has just the hint of lemon to make it extra special.

Cake Ingredients:

6 large eggs at room temperature
2 cups of sugar
2 cups of all-purpose flour
1 tablespoon of baking powder
5 tablespoons of finely shredded coconut
1 cup (2 sticks) of melted butter
1 lemon zest

Directions:

Preheat oven to 350° F and grease a 10x4 tube or bundt pan.

Separate the eggs in two separate bowls. Beat the egg whites on high until they form high peaks then leave aside. Beat egg yolks with sugar and melted butter; gradually add the flour and baking powder. Begin to fold in the egg whites, lemon zest and coconut. Pour into pan and bake for 1 hour.

After the cake comes out of the oven wait for just a few minutes and remove from pan to serving plate. Make sure the serving plate is a little bit bigger than the cake, because of the next step.

Glaze Topping:

1 cup of milk
1 cup of sugar

Directions:

Heat 1 cup of milk with 1 cup of sugar and stir until the sugar dissolves. Then, prick holes over the cake using a toothpick and slowly pour the glaze topping mixture over the warm cake. The cake will absorb everything, which is the secret as to why this cake is so moist. Lastly, decorate with shredded coconut over the top of the cake. I promise, if you love coconut and lemon this will be your favorite cake too!

Other Favorites

fresh cheese

Queijo Fresco

Ingredients:
1 gallon of whole milk
2 teaspoons powdered rennet
4 round cheese molds, each 4 ½-inches in diameter
Sea salt to taste

Directions:
Over low heat, warm the milk until it is lukewarm, about 97° F. It is very important not to overheat it. Once it's lukewarm, add the powered rennet and mix well. Remove pan from heat and wait 30-45 minutes for the milk to coagulate and begin to form curds. At this time, place each mold on an individual plate and make sure the plates have a nice lip so they can hold the excess whey that will release over time.

When the milk coagulates, use a slotted spoon to fill the molds with the curds. As the curds stay in the mold, liquid (whey) will come out of the openings. You have to be careful to discard the whey while keeping the curds safely in the mold. I also make sure to press down the curds with the spoon; this usually helps to remove more of the whey and creates a firmer cheese.

Sprinkle sea salt to taste and refrigerate overnight. This is when most of the whey will drain.

The following morning, place another plate over your mold and flip it upside down over a sink to drain out all of the excess whey that has collected. Then, place the plate back in the refrigerator to sit for another 24 hours. It should be ready to eat by the third day.

I think the longer it stays in the fridge and the more whey is released, the better the cheese firms to the consistency I like. This fresh cheese tastes great with crushed red pepper sauce, and it's customary to serve this soft cheese on fresh or toasted bread.

Note: Make sure to use local milk that isn't double pasteurized. This might affect the milk coagulating. Also, when storing, make sure it's in sealed containers since soft cheese is very high in moisture and small amounts of whey will continue to be released.

To view the how-to video with step-by-step instructions, please go to youtube.com/azoreangreenbean.

salted and crushed red hot peppers

Pimentas Salgadas e Moídas

Every fall my dad would have cases of red hot peppers delivered to our home. The process was the same every year. He would prepare enough so that my mom would use it to cook all of our meals throughout the year. As his daughters married his batches became bigger and bigger each year in order to have enough to share with all of us. We could all go out and buy some off the selves in our local Portuguese markets but it was never as good as my dad's. He was very meticulous about removing the seeds as well as hand grinding the peppers to the perfect consistency. It was always a huge treat to get my year's supply delivered by him...oh how I miss that. I can still see him now in his yellow heavy-duty gloves, being careful not to touch his face, grinding away and filling the jars. At the end of the night he would be soaking his hands in milk, since he touched some of the peppers and his hands would have a burning sensation. Writing all of this down, I can't imagine why anyone would want to go to these lengths for homemade crushed red peppers. But he did it every year, it was tradition. Unfortunately none of his daughters have continued this tradition. So when a friend or extended family member makes it, we feel like someone has delivered gold to our door when they show up with a jar of the crushed hot red peppers!

The recipe below comes from my brother-in-law Ernest who would help my dad when he would allow any help. I haven't given any specific amount regarding how many peppers to buy. That is up to you depending if you want to experiment with a pound or two, before you start ordering cases and making enough for your whole family.

Salted peppers:

Ingredients:
Red hot finger peppers, about 6" to 8" long
Coarse sea salt
Large and deep lidded glass or ceramic container

Directions:
Carefully wash all the peppers and blot them dry.

Cut them in half and deseed each pepper. Layer them in the container and cover each layer with salt. Continue this until you fill up the container or run out of peppers.

Cover and store in a cool dark place for about 2-3 weeks. Don't be discouraged if after those weeks some of the peppers turned a little darker or softer. This is all normal and don't think it needs to be refrigerated either, the peppers are well preserved in the salt.

Save some of these preserved peppers in mason jars and use them sliced alongside many dishes. Then the remaining peppers will be hand-ground for our pimenta moida, adding that extra flavor and heat into pretty much all our meals.

Crushed peppers:
After the salted peppers are done, my dad would hand grind them to the perfect size and consistency. Being careful not to get any of the oils from the pepper onto your skin, you need to make sure you wear protective gloves as well as even safety glasses to protect your eyes. My dad would blot the salted peppers to remove any excess salt. Then he would grind them using a hand cranking grinder setup attached to a table with a bowl to catch the crushed peppers. Then once again he filled up a very large ceramic container with the crushed peppers. This process took a very long time. He would then cover it, and let it all rest for a few days. Then once he was ready he would have my mom sterilize the mason jars. Once that was done he would fill the jars almost to the very top with the crushed peppers, and fill the remaining space in the jar with olive oil. The jars would be covered and stored in a cool dark space.

That was my dad's way of doing it, but now my brother-in-law said when he makes a small batch he pretty much does everything except use the hand cranking grinder. Instead he places the salted peppers in a food processor and slowly adds olive oil until the mix is to the consistency he likes. He also keeps his batches refrigerated instead of in the pantry.

marinades and sauces

Marinadas e Molhos

Marinade for Beef or Pork:

Ingredients:
1 cup of red or white wine
½ teaspoon of cinnamon (My mom would always use cinnamon especially in her beef dishes)
1 or 2 teaspoons of crushed garlic
1 teaspoon of dry crushed red pepper
1 small rough chopped onion
Salt and pepper to taste

Directions:
Put the meat of choice in a large bowl. Mix all of the ingredients and pour over the meat. Mix everything together very well, making sure every part of the meat is coated. Cover and let it marinate overnight in the refrigerator for best flavoring.

Sauce for Fish:
Molho de Vilao / Villain Sauce

Ingredients:
½ cup of red table wine
½ cup of wine vinegar
1 cup of olive oil
1 onion, chopped fine thin slices
2 cloves garlic, crushed and chopped
1 hot red pepper cut into thin strips*
*can substitute with 1 tablespoon of chopped red hot pepper sauce
1 bunch of parsley, chopped
Salt to taste
1 teaspoon of safflower or paprika

Directions:
In a bowl add the chopped onion, garlic, pepper and salt. Add wine, vinegar and olive oil, then mix everything and let it rest a bit to get a taste. Add parsley and safflower, before pouring the sauce over the layers of cooked fish and serve.

This recipe is enough for 1 lb of fish. Increase the amounts depending on how many pounds of fish you'll be serving.

Molho Cru / Raw Sauce

Ingredients:

½ onion, chopped
3 garlic cloves, chopped
2 tablespoons of olive oil
2 tablespoons of chopped red hot pepper sauce
1 teaspoon of wine vinegar
1 small bunch of fresh parsley, chopped

Directions:

In a bowl add all of the ingredients, mix everything together and keep refrigerated. This sauce is to be used cold and can be poured over any fried or grilled fish.

Marinada de vinho e alho / Wine and garlic marinade

Ingredients:

2 cups of burgundy wine
2 cloves of garlic, chopped
1 tablespoon of paprika
1 tablespoon of crushed red hot pepper sauce
Salt to taste

Directions:

This is a ratio of the marinade, and can be doubled depending on how much meat is being used in your recipe. Make sure meat is covered with marinade and refrigerated at least overnight before cooking.

liqueurs

Licores

On my last visit to Sao Miguel I had the pleasure of having a very memorable dinner at my cousin João Manuel's home with his lovely family. We had the customary late dinner that didn't start until 8:00 pm and it was nearing midnight when we were offered some homemade liqueur to help our stomach digest. It was then I had the most delicious tangerine liqueur, followed by orange, then pineapple. Yes it was an evening of remembering days gone by and retelling those stories that made us laugh to the wee hours of the morning. In one of those stories João Manuel told me that my mother was also very good at making liqueur, a fact I was never aware of until that moment. He said she would often have an assortment of tangerine, lemon, pineapple and milk liqueurs during the Christmas season to offer to all of her visitors. I loved hearing the stories of how my dad would make the wine in the fall, and from the leftover grape skins he made moonshine so my mom could make her liqueurs. At that moment I knew I would be making my own liqueurs as well to share with my family and friends.

The recipe João Manuel gave me can be used with all citrus fruit peels. Since all the fruits were typically picked fresh and in season it's best to use organic fruits. The alcohol will extract the color and flavor of the peels so the liqueur has to be as pure as possible with no added chemicals. I experimented with lemons and then with navel oranges, and all I can say is that they were both delicious.

Orange or Lemon Liqueur

Ingredients:

4 cups grain alcohol
2 lbs organic oranges or lemons
6 cups water
4 cups sugar

Directions:

Peel the orange or lemon skins very thinly so that only the top part of the skin is peeled. Be careful to avoid the white part of the rind, as it will make the liqueur bitter.

Soak the skins in the alcohol in a large glass container. Make sure the skins are completely submerged. Seal the container with a lid and let it stand for a minimum of 14 days.

After the peels have soaked, strain the peels from the alcohol. If the skins have broken up into very small pieces, use a coffee filter in your strainer to help catch all the loose pieces. Throw away the peels and set the orange or lemon-infused alcohol aside.

In a separate pan, bring the water to a boil. Add the sugar and stir until it has dissolved, making a simple syrup. Cover the pan and set aside until it has cooled to room temperature (at least a few hours).

Once the simple syrup mixture has reached room temperature, mix in the orange or lemon flavored alcohol. At this time you are now ready to bottle.

I was able to fill two 750 mL sized bottles (typical wine bottle size) and a couple of smaller bottles as well. How to store and serve the liqueur is up to your preference. In Sao Miguel, it was served at room temperature, but I personally prefer it chilled from the freezer.

pineapple jam

Doce de Ananás

One of the great things about visiting a traditional Azorean greenhouse plantation of pineapples is that you get to meet the owners. I was very lucky to meet Estuferio José Soares and his wife Filomena. José reviewed all the workings of the plantation, but Filomena shared with me all the traditional pineapple recipes. Pineapple jam is served in the morning with an array of other homemade fruit jams along with toast but I love this jam any time of the day. It's simply delicious and easy to make.

This recipe makes 4 cups of jam, but the recipe is also very easy to double if you're planning on making enough for gift giving.

Ingredients:
2 lbs of crushed pineapple
1 ½ lbs of granulated sugar

Directions:
Buy a whole pineapple. (Yes, you can buy canned pineapple but you want as organic as you can get in making this traditional jam.) In choosing your fresh pineapple you will need to use your sense of smell––the pineapple must smell highly aromatic, namely sweet and fresh. If you detect an odor or there is no sweetness present, skip that pineapple. Also avoid pineapples that are bruised or mushy to the touch.

Place the pineapple on its side and cut the crown and the stem off the pineapple. Stand the pineapple up on one end and using a very sharp knife slice off the sides, going from top to bottom. Leave as much flesh as possible remaining on the pineapple––by following the contour of the fruit, this will help to prevent loss of flesh where the pineapple bulges in the middle. Next, remove the eye spots. I find using the end of a potato peeler helps in removing the eye spots. Now you're ready to cut the pineapple into halves, then quarters for cubes or wedges. For each quarter, cut off the core before cutting further into chunks, then cut the chunks to size. For this jam you'll want to cut into very small chunks and then using a mallet, crush the pineapple chucks.

Once all the pineapple is crushed you're going to weigh out 2 lbs and place into a 4 quart heavy bottom saucepan. Add the 1 ½ lbs of sugar and mix well together. Continue to stir on a medium heat until it's brought to a boil. Then lower the heat and continue to stir until all liquid is absorbed to your liking.

I stirred for about one hour and still left a little syrup liquid to keep the jam moist. Also since this recipe has no preservatives, you must store it in the refrigerator and it will keep for several weeks.

harvest time

Vindimas

Harvest time, or as we would say vindimas, was in September and it was one of the most fun seasons growing up. My dad had a vineyard in Sao Miguel so when we emigrated to the U.S. he made sure the wine making tradition continued except here in the U.S. he would have to order all his grapes from California. I remember having so many crates of grapes delivered to our home and for what felt like months became winemaking central with weekend parties at our home. Since I was young, and a girl, my job was to stay upstairs with the women cooking lots of food for the men downstairs in our basement. My favorite memory was when I followed my grandmother down to the basement…she showed me the piles of grapes being sorted, the pressing and the new wine that I could taste. It was sweet grape juice, but I thought I was given

wine. After all the work came the eating, the laughing and the singing. In the years that followed it was the same routine every September. My dad would have his wine in a couple of wooden barrels and he prided himself in his wine, making sure that every guest in our home would get to sample his yearly vintage.

As my father became older he stopped making wine but on his last visit to Sao Miguel he was able to make wine with his brothers one last time. Even though two had passed before then I have a feeling they were all together. It was the happiest I have ever seen him. I am so happy that I have these pictures.

grape jelly

Doce de Uva

I think part of coming to the United States was the understanding that we never wanted to forget where we came from. My dad had a plantation in Sao Miguel that contained a very large navel orange grove as well as a vineyard; it was second nature for us to always have a grape arbor in our backyard. I loved nothing more than sitting under the arbor with my dad and breathing the sweet smell of the grapes as they were ripening. We would also sneak a few before dinner time, too. In the fall my dad would continue the family tradition of making wine and my mom making her grape jelly. Every fall I head over to my parents' old home, which is still in the family, and I sit under the grape arbor and think of all the great memories. Then I take my basket and pick some grapes off the vine. Once the basket is filled I know I have about 5 lbs of grapes and enough extra for my family to enjoy.

I have two recipes for jelly. One came from my Aunt Ines, who likes to use the white grapes she has growing on her arbor to make white grape jelly. Her recipe makes a small batch compared to the recipe from my Aunt Lilia, which produces a large batch that yields 6 lbs of jelly.

Tia Ines – White Grape Jelly Recipe

Ingredients:

2 lbs of white grapes
2 lbs of granulated sugar

Directions:

In a large saucepan add the washed grapes and over medium heat keep stirring the grapes until they break apart and bring it to a boil. Then remove from heat and cool completely. Once it's cooled completely, strain out the seeds and skin.

Add the strained grapes back into the saucepan and add the sugar. Over medium heat, keep stirring until it reaches the thickness in consistency that you like. You don't want to overcook it, since the jelly will harden as it cools.

Aunt Lilia - Grape Jelly

Ingredients:

5 lbs of grapes
5 lbs of granulated sugar

Directions:

In a large stockpot add the washed grapes and the sugar, and over medium heat bring to a simmer. The grapes will begin to pop and break open. Continue stirring the grapes as they break apart and begin to turn a pinkish color with foam forming on top. If this happens quickly you will need to lower the heat and continue to stir. Then slowly the color will deepen and the jelly will start to thicken. Once you have it to your liking in thickness, strain out the seeds and peels.

Pour the strained jelly into sterilized mason jars. This recipe yielded 6 lbs of jelly, enough to have for my whole family and still give some away to friends. Keep stored in the refrigerator.

fig jam

Doce de Figos

I love figs; fresh or dried, they are wonderful. But jam brings the taste of figs up to a different level. The first time I had fig jam was when my Aunt Lilia served it with some sharp cheeses and some curried meats. Then when I visited Sao Miguel, my cousin Laureana served it for breakfast on toast along with some Sao Jorge cheese on the side. Both times the sweet jam along with the sharp and salty meats and cheeses made for a wonderful combination.

This recipe came from my Aunt Lilia. The recipe uses fresh figs, but since they have a short window of availability she sometimes uses dried figs in the recipe. They do have a different consistency than the fresh ones, but it's still delicious.

This recipe yields 4 cups of jam.

Ingredients:

4 cups of firm fresh figs (any type)
4 cups of granulated sugar
2 tablespoons lemon juice

Directions:

Rinse well and cut the figs. Depending on size you may want to quarter or cut in half. Put the cut figs into a large saucepan, and add 2 cups of the sugar.

At medium to high heat, bring to a boil and let boil for about 10 minutes, stirring constantly. Add lemon juice and the rest of the sugar.

Bring to a boil again, using a wooden spoon to constantly stir until the sugar becomes a syrup and then a thicker gel. Once it's reached the consistency that you like, remove from heat. Make sure to occasionally stir while the jam is cooling off.

While cooling, take out the fig skins with tongs. (This makes it a jam, leaving the skins in makes it a preserve.)

When the jam has completely cooled off, pour into sterilized mason jars.

Sometimes, you may want to let this stand overnight before putting it into jars. Since fruit will float when it's hot, the jars end up with fruit on top and syrup on the bottom. But if you stir while it's cooling, that helps with it as well.

Store jars in refrigerator, and it will keep for 2 months.

roasted chestnuts

Castanhas Assadas

Growing up, chestnuts meant the beginning of November and the feast of Sao Martinho. This feast is held on November 11th and everyone celebrates by cooking and eating roasted chestnuts; my dad would take over the kitchen on this day. He would shop for fresh chestnuts; some came directly from Portugal and others from Spain, and buying them was always fun. He would show me a healthy chestnut and explain that they needed to be unwrinkled with a glossy brown surface. If they weren't it could mean they had mold inside. He would also show me how some would have small pinholes in them; you want to avoid those too, since that meant that worms have been drilling. So it became like a treasure hunt, with me picking one up and getting his approval if it was ok or not.

Then we would take the bag full of chestnuts home and I would watch him prepare it.

Directions:

Using 1 lb of fresh chestnuts, rinse them well and using a very sharp knife, carefully make an incision the shape of an X at the bottom of each nut, making sure it's deep enough to cut through the shell, and just into the flesh of the nut. This will allow steam to escape, otherwise the chestnuts can explode!

After slitting the shells, transfer the chestnuts to a saucepan and add enough cold water to cover. Bring the water to a boil for about 10-15 minutes. Then strain out the water, and transfer the chestnuts to a roasting pan or cast iron skillet, and roast them in a 350° F oven for about 30 minutes. Remove from oven and start peeling.

It's important to start peeling the chestnuts while they are hot. Remove and discard each shell and the papery skin. Some will come off easy, some will not. It's really not you, it's the chestnut. Sometimes you might need to use your fingernails to pick the papery skin. It does become more difficult as they cool off; if that happens you can quickly reheat them in the oven.

tea plantations in sao miguel

Plantações de Chá de São Miguel

We are very lucky in Sao Miguel to have not one but two tea plantations. The original plantation is called Gorreana Tea and the second is called Porto Formosa Tea; these are actually the only tea plantations to be found in all of Europe. I'm definitely not going to give a history of tea by any means but I can tell you that the tea was brought to the island from Macau, China in the mid-19th Century around 1883. Even today, they are still using the same methods that were taught back then and produce, in my opinion, the best organic black and green tea.

My family members are big tea drinkers. Don't get me wrong, coffee would always be served in the morning, but tea would be served the rest of the day, whether for a mid-afternoon break or before bedtime. My parent's favorite tea was the black loose leaf Gorreana Tea. I can honestly say that Gorreana has been my family's tea of choice for more than 100 years.

One of the first places I visit when I am in Sao Miguel is these two tea plantations. If you happen to visit in the summer you might be lucky to see them harvest the crop. But any time of the year I would recommend a visit. Plus, you don't ever want to miss their tea rooms for sampling the different teas; then you can decide your favorite between the black, green or the orange pekoe.

Chá
Porto Formoso
CHÁ GORREANA

regional ceramic pottery

Cerâmica Reginal

One of my favorite stops when visiting Sao Miguel is Cerâmica Vieira. I make sure I rush over on the same day that I land, that way if I want any pottery to be personalized it gives them a week to complete the special order. Of course if you're not looking at special orders you can buy from a huge selection that they have in their showroom. You can even walk through their factory and see them working at the different stages of production, from working with the clay on the wheel to the end result. I especially love to watch them paint each piece by hand. Everything is made the same since they were founded in 1862 in Lagoa. You can not leave the Island without dropping in and picking up a few of their beautiful pieces of functional art.

index

kitchen measurement conversion tables

Liquid or Volume Measures (approximate)

1 teaspoon		1/3 tablespoon	5 ml
1 tablespoon	1/2 fluid ounce	3 teaspoons	15 ml, 15 cc
2 tablespoons	1 fluid ounce	1/8 cup, 6 teaspoons	30 ml, 30 cc
1/4 cup	2 fluid ounces	4 tablespoons	59 ml
1/3 cup	2 2/3 fluid ounces	5 tablespoons & 1 teaspoon	79 ml
1/2 cup	4 fluid ounces	8 tablespoons	118 ml
2/3 cup	5 1/3 fluid ounces	10 tablespoons & 2 teaspoons	158 ml
3/4 cup	6 fluid ounces	12 tablespoons	177 ml
7/8 cup	7 fluid ounces	14 tablespoons	207 ml
1 cup	8 fluid ounces/ 1/2 pint	16 tablespoons	237 ml
2 cups	16 fluid ounces/ 1 pint	32 tablespoons	473 ml
4 cups	32 fluid ounces	1 quart	946 ml
1 pint	16 fluid ounces/ 1 pint	32 tablespoons	473 ml
2 pints	32 fluid ounces	1 quart	946 ml, 0.946 liters
8 pints	1 gallon/ 128 fluid ounces	4 quarts	3785 ml, 3.78 liters
4 quarts	1 gallon/128 fluid ounces	1 gallon	3785 ml, 3.78 liters
1 liter	1.057 quarts		1000 ml
1 gallon	4 quarts	128 fluid ounces	3785 ml, 3.78 liters

Dry Or Weight Measurements (approximate)

1 ounce	30 grams (28.35 g)	
2 ounces	55 grams	
3 ounces	85 grams	
4 ounces	1/4 pound	125 grams
8 ounces	1/2 pound	240 grams
12 ounces	3/4 pound	375 grams
16 ounces	1 pound	454 grams
32 ounces	2 pounds	907 grams
1/4 pound	4 ounces	125 grams
1/2 pound	8 ounces	240 grams
3/4 pound	12 ounces	375 grams
1 pound	16 ounces	454 grams
2 pounds	32 ounces	907 grams
1 kilogram	2.2 pounds/ 35.2 ounces	1000 grams